Y0-DKF-305

International Business Reference Sources

The LexingtonBooks Special Series in Libraries and Librarianship

Richard D. Johnson, General Editor

The Parliament of Great Britain: A Bibliography
Robert U. Goehlert and *Fenton S. Martin*

Prizewinning Books for Children
Jaqueline Shachter Weiss

The Feminization of Librarianship in France
Mary Niles Maack

The Public Library in the 1980s
Lawrence J. White

International Business Reference Sources
Cynthia C. Ryans

Vietnam War Bibliography
Christopher L. Sugnet and *John Hickey*

The Electronic Library
Hugh F. Cline and *Loraine T. Sinnott*

Archival Choices
Nancy E. Peace

International Business Reference Sources

Developing a Corporate Library

Cynthia C. Ryans
Kent State University

LexingtonBooks
D.C. Heath and Company
Lexington, Massachusetts
Toronto

Library of Congress Cataloging in Publication Data
Ryans, Cynthia C., 1933–
International business reference sources.

Includes index.
1. Commerce—Bibliography. 2. Export sales—Bibliography. 3. International business enterprises—Bibliography. I. Title.
Z7164.C8R9 1983 [HF1008] 016.658′049 82-49323
ISBN 0-669-06612-5

Second printing, August 1984

Published simultaneously in Canada

Printed in the United States of America on acid-free paper

International Standard Book Number: 0-669-06612-5

Library of Congress Catalog Card Number: 82-49323

For John

Contents

Foreword

The sine qua non of world trade is information—data on market size, buying preferences, distribution channels, available distributors and agents; statistics on financial and economic conditions, trends, and indicators. U.S. exporters and those who seek to facilitate their important and difficult task need information on all these areas—and much more. U.S. exporters seeking information on foreign countries, unfortunately, face many hurdles—lack of familiarity with foreign information sources, incomparability of data, and often language barriers. Further, few countries offer the wealth of data, through both private and government agencies, that executives are accustomed to using in making business decisions.

Cynthia Ryans, a respected international librarian and bibliographer, has performed yeoman's work for this book. Her efforts should be of considerable benefit to business executives, to corporate research librarians, to international banks, and to the marketing-research departments of large multinational corporations. This book will be the authority on information sources for conducting international business. It deserves a place not on the shelf but on the desk of international marketing and overseas-business-development executives.

Ryans is a well-established professional bibliographer with an excellent reputation in the international area. It is certain that the quality and usefulness of this book will extend her reputation as an authority in the field of world trade sources. I congratulate her on the quality of this work and express the hope that many companies will benefit from it.

Ivan R. Vernon, Director
World Trade Education Center
Cleveland State University

Acknowledgments

Many people have helped me at various stages in the development of this project, and I would first like to thank the publishers and distributors who supplied me with current information on the publications included here. This book would not have been possible without their assistance. In addition, I would like to thank Dr. Ivan Vernon for preparing the foreword for this book.

There are several people who have been a great help to me in the preparation of the manuscript. Janet Gifford not only typed the entire manuscript but also performed many other important and necessary tasks involved in completing this project. In addition, Ron Dornan was a great help in preparing the information for the final typing, and Linda Poje assisted in proofreading.

Most important, I wish to thank my husband, Dr. John K. Ryans, Jr., for his continued assistance and encouragement throughout this entire project.

Introduction

A suggested solution for overcoming the difficulties of foreign marketing research: . . . "Gather information from as many sources as possible. Develop and maintain up-to-date company records and libraries."[1]

The interest in international business among U.S. firms has grown dramatically in the past decade or so, and it has undoubtedly been heightened by the rapid increase in the number of foreign manufacturers (and foreign direct involvement in the United States) that has occurred since 1978. In fact, the total foreign direct investment in the United States reached $89.8 billion in 1981, an increase of 31 percent over the preceding year.[2]

On the other hand, American multinationals (MNCs) have long been active in foreign markets, and total overseas investments by the corporations reached an estimated $227.3 billion in 1981.[3] But it is now the small- to medium-sized firms that are exploring ways to sell their products overseas. Their method of entry may be through wholly owned subsidiaries as many MNCs have historically preferred, but realistically they are more likely to employ joint ventures, licensing agreements, foreign sales offices, or exporting. While licensing fees and royalties paid to the U.S. companies reached $5.9 billion in 1981,[4] for example, it is exporting that initially attracts most firms of this size. Federal and state governmental bodies have added their weight to this exporting impetus by offering a variety of special programs to aid the beginning exporter, as well as encouraging/stimulating the veteran traders to place more emphasis on foreign markets.

As more and more companies turn their attention overseas both to take advantage of the natural opportunities for selling their products and/or services *and* to hedge against domestic fluctuations, their needs for information rise sharply. However, conducting primary research overseas is costly and "every method of primary data collection faces severe limitations in foreign countries due to differences in cultures, languages, attitudes, customs, levels of literacy, postal services, and communications and transportation facilities."[5] A firm's first informational efforts must therefore be focused on secondary sources.

Consequently, company libraries, public libraries, and college and university libraries all have found that there is an increased demand for international business sources. This book was developed to assist in meeting this demand, especially to provide a single source of representative holdings.

An International Perspective

Why did it take so long for the bulk of U.S. firms to become interested in overseas markets, and why do even veteran business people need international "basics"? First, without being redundant, it is necessary to emphasize that international business is quite different from domestic business. Second, there have been many specific reasons for this lack of interest overseas by business people. One, for example, concerns the perceived high risk many firms associate with marketing a product overseas. (A widely publicized devaluation of the Mexican peso that caused some firms to incur major losses reinforced the fears of business people and made them reluctant to deal abroad.)

Perhaps the fear of terrorism has kept some companies from entering the overseas market. However, a more likely (and quite simple) reason is that the firm managers and owners lack the knowledge and experience needed in exporting and determining which foreign markets offer the greatest potential. They are unaware that a wealth of information is available through secondary resources that can often be obtained at little or no expense to the company.

The obvious sources, which the researcher may go to first, include the Department of Commerce, International Trade Administration; the Organisation for Economic Cooperation and Development; The International Monetary Fund publications; and The World Bank. However, there are still many other well-known sources as well as some very useful sources that are not necessarily familiar to the international businessman.

Thus this book is designed to assist in providing the needed international perspective that so many firms (and business people) lack. The content is not limited to exporting but relates to any form of foreign-market entry a firm may choose. Experienced internationalists, on the other hand, will likely find new information sources.

For Whom the Book is Intended

The book is mainly directed toward the U.S. businessman doing business abroad, either through exporting or some other form of entry. It can be used on an individual basis or as a main tool for either setting up a company library or adding to an already existing library. In addition, there are many foreign businesses and libraries who rely heavily on U.S. international business materials, and this bibliography can be a very useful reference source for them.

According to the new American Assembly of Collegiate Schools of Business guidelines, many business schools are now developing or expanding their international business programs. In order to support these programs, they will need to expand their library holdings. This guide will assist them in their library material selection.

The book is also intended to be a supplementary text to courses in two areas of graduate study. In addition to the graduate international business program, this book can provide a very useful source of additional information to the library science student in the business bibliography course.

Purpose of the Book

This book presents a representative list of the more essential sources of information useful to companies involved in doing business overseas. However, the intent is not to list every available source but rather the ones that are most useful to the majority of international businesses. Therefore the items chosen for inclusion typically are general in nature; that is, they are neither industry, company, nor country specific. However, there are a few titles of a specific nature, such as those on specific industrial groups or products, which are included to show the reader that information on most products does exist and further research by the business person can result in finding more information on his or her specific product or country of interest.

There is an abundance of information available on every country in the world. Of course, it would be much too cumbersome to list all this information in a single book. Therefore, the author has chosen to include only those sources that cover (or are applicable) in many countries and in a few cases, those that cover the countries where the majority of overseas business is currently being conducted. Again, there are a few items included for some of the smaller countries but only to give the reader an idea of what type of material is available and from where it can be obtained.

A number of very useful foreign publications can be obtained from foreign embassies, councils, and economic-development offices. However, this information varies in quality and availability so it is not being included in this book. Only brief mention is made of a few foreign sources. The book deals primarily with domestic sources. However, there are lists in the appendix of foreign publishers and other foreign sources.

On-Line Data Bases

One of the most recent means of searching current material is through an on-line data base. While this method is very useful to the researcher, many of the data bases focus more on journal articles than on actual sourcebooks. There is, however, quite a bit of statistical information available through data bases, so this source should not be overlooked as research material. The detail of the contents of data bases is much too great to include in a single book, and thus the author has chosen not to include them in this book. However, the reader should be aware that these services are available and can be obtained through many local, public, and college and university libraries as well as through some businesses. Although it is often expensive to have such a system in-house, some companies do have these computer facilities and can add more data bases as they become available.

Format

For the convenience of the reader, the book is divided into four main sections: government publications; subscription services (journals, loose-leaf services, annuals, and so on); international business data sources (directories, statistical material, almanacs, and so on); and general international business books (marketing, finance, economics, and so on). Within each category, the material is arranged alphabetically by title including pertinent information for each title. It should be kept in mind here that it is important for international businesses to have the most current information available. Thus it is necessary that organizations develop a working system for subscription services that will ensure that they are received on a regular basis. Monitoring such a system is very important, and it is recommended that a filing system be developed to ensure that each title is renewed on time (where no on-line system is used).

Each citation includes the title of the book and the address where the piece can be ordered. In addition, other information is given when available: the number of pages in the book or the frequency of publication, the price, the Library of Congress Call Number, and at least one subject heading. Most titles are self-explanatory. However, a brief description has been given for some titles to further clarify their contents.

The prices listed are those that were quoted at the time the book was written. Prices on printed material are constantly changing so the prices quoted here may not always be current. In addition, the prices given here are the retail list prices. Many companies and organizations offer discounts on their publications: some for memberships, educational discounts, and so on. Therefore, if the company ordering the book qualifies for any one of the many discounts available, the price could be considerably less than what is quoted here. Prices were unavailable for some items. There are a few titles included that can be obtained free.

The addresses included with each title generally represent the publisher of the piece. In some cases, however, a distributor is listed. There are also foreign publications that can be obtained through an American distributor, and the American address is provided here. For more information on other titles available and more information on the pieces mentioned in this book, the reader can contact the address listed for each title.

In addition, some journals change their names over the years. A researcher may be familiar with a journal and not be able to find it listed here. It may be that the name has been changed. In addition, new editions of books are often published under a different title or the same book may be published in the United States and in another country under different titles. Throughout this book, previous titles and multititles of publications are listed and cross-references included from the old title to the current title.

Often the international business person needs the most current references available to further assist him or her. The author has included a list of publishers and organizations in the appendix that can provide further update information and country-specific data. In addition, a brief list and explanation of the Department of Commerce programs available to international business people has been included to provide the reader with an idea of the services available to exporters by this organization.

Notes

1. Vinay Kothari, "Strengthening Foreign Marketing Programs," in *Contemporary Perspectives in International Business*, Harold W. Berkman and Ivan R. Vernon eds. (Chicago: Rand McNally College Publishing Company, 1979), p. 194.
2. Ned G. Howenstine and Gregory G. Fouch, "Foreign Direct Investment in the United States in 1981," *Survey of Current Business*, August 1982, p. 30.
3. Obie G. Whichard, "U.S. Direct Investment Abroad in 1981," *Survey of Current Business*, August 1982, p. 11.
4. Ibid., p. 29.
5. Kothari, "Strengthening Foreign Marketing Programs," p. 193.

1 Government Publications

Agriculture Supply & Demand Estimates see **World Agricultural Supply and Demand Estimates.**

Antitrust Guide for International Operations
United States Department of Justice, Antitrust Division.
1977. rev. ed. 63p. $2.75.
Subject heading: Antitrust law—United States
Library of Congress Call Number: KF1652 .J87

Contains a general description of antitrust enforcement policy in the international sector. Useful for business decision makers, lawyers, and others concerned with international antitrust legislation.
Superintendent of Documents
U.S. Government Printing Office
Washington, DC 20402
(202) 275–2051

Background Notes
United States Department of State, Bureau of Public Affairs.
Annual. $18.00.
Subject heading: Geography—Collections
Library of Congress Call Number: G59 .U5

Contains profiles of numerous countries worldwide, providing up-to-date information on the country, the economy, government, people, geography, history, principal government officials, travel notes, and so on.
Superintendent of Documents
U.S. Government Printing Office
Washington, DC 20402
(202) 275–2051

Background Notes, Index
United States Department of State, Bureau of Public Affairs.
Semiannual. $1.90.
Subject heading: Geography—Index
Superintendent of Documents
U.S. Government Printing Office
Washington, DC 20402
(202) 275–2051

A Basic Guide to Exporting

United States Department of Commerce, International Trade Administration.
1981. 133p. $3.25.
Subject heading: Export marketing—United States—Handbooks, manuals, etc.
Library of Congress Call Number: HF1009.5 .B344 1981

This book is intended as a guide for firms new in the exporting field.
Superintendent of Documents
U.S. Government Printing Office
Washington, DC 20402
(202) 275–2051

Business America

United States Department of Commerce, International Trade Administration.
Biweekly. $55.00/year.
Subject heading: United States—commerce—Periodicals
Library of Congress Call Number: HF1 .B863

Articles concerning international business opportunities and commerce are featured in this all-purpose journal of trade and international business.
Superintendent of Documents
U.S. Government Printing Office
Washington, DC 20402
(202) 275–2051

A Business Guide to the Near East & North Africa

United States Department of Commerce, International Trade Administration.
1980. $4.50.

Contains pertinent information for doing business in the following countries: Algeria, Bahrain, Egypt, Iraq, Israel, Jordan, Kuwait, Lebanon, Libya, Morocco, Oman, People's Democratic Republic of Yemen, Qatar, Saudi Arabia, Syria, Tunisia, United Arab Emirates, and Yemen Arab Republic.
Superintendent of Documents
U.S. Government Printing Office
Washington, DC 20402
(202) 275–2051

Business Today see **Business America.**

Commerce America see **Business America.**

Commerce Publications Update
United States Department of Commerce.
Biweekly. $22.00/year.
Subject heading: United States—Department of Commerce—Bibliography—Periodicals

Newsletter that announces recent publications of the U.S. Department of Commerce, including reports, pamphlets, charts, periodicals, and news releases. Provides titles, prices, ordering instructions, and annotations where appropriate.
Superintendent of Documents
U.S. Government Printing Office
Washington, DC 20402
(202) 275–2051

Commerce Today see **Business America.**

Countertrade Practices in East Europe, The Soviet Union and China: An Introductory Guide to Business
Pompiliu Verzariu.
1980. 102p.
Subject heading: East-West Trade (1945–)
Library of Congress Call Number: HF1411 .V444 1980
U.S. Department of Commerce
International Trade Administration
Washington, DC 20230
(202) 377–2000

Country Labor Profiles
Irregular. Free.
Subject heading: Labor and laboring classes—Collected works.

Statistical information on forty countries.
Division of Foreign Labor Statistics and Trade
Bureau of Labor Statistics
Washington, DC 20210
(202) 523–8165

Country Market Sectoral Surveys
Price varies.
Subject heading: Market surveys

Contains detailed market surveys of export opportunities to U.S. trade

partners. At the present time surveys have been conducted on Brazil, Indonesia, Nigeria, Venezuela, Japan, and Iran.
Superintendent of Documents
U.S. Government Printing Office
Washington, DC 20402
(202) 275–2051

Customs Regulations of the United States
United States Customs Service.
1981. Loose leaf for updating. $32.00.
Subject heading: Customs administration—United States

Consists of regulations developed and published for the purpose of carrying out customs laws supervised by the Bureau of Customs.
Superintendent of Documents
U.S. Government Printing Office
Washington, DC 20402
(202) 275–2051

Diplomatic List
Quarterly. $12.00.
Subject heading: Diplomatic and consular service in the United States—Directories
Library of Congress Call Number: JX1705 .A22

Officers (including commercial attachés) of foreign embassies and legations in Washington, DC., are listed.
Superintendent of Documents
U.S. Government Printing Office
Washington, DC 20402
(202) 275–2051

Electric Current Abroad
1975–1980. $2.00.
Subject heading: Electric currents—Directories
Library of Congress Call Number: TK12 .E35

Contains pertinent information concerning the characteristics of electric current available and the type of attachment plugs used in principal cities worldwide.
Superintendent of Documents
U.S. Government Printing Office
Washington, DC 20402
(202) 275–2051

European Trade Fairs: A Guide for Exporters

L.R. Thomas.

1981. 81p. $4.25.

Subject heading: Europe—Fairs—Directories

Provides easy-to-follow instructions on how to successfully participate in European trade fairs. In addition, it lists and indexes major trade fairs by product categories.

Superintendent of Documents
U.S. Government Printing Office
Washington, DC 20402
(202) 275–2051

Export Administration Bulletin see **The Export Administration Regulations.**

The Export Administration Regulations

$105.00.

Subject heading: Export controls—United States
Library of Congress Call Number: KF1987 .A329 .045

Provides detailed explanations of U.S. export-licensing requirements. Also, subscribers receive *Export Administration Bulletins*, which explain recent policy changes and furnish replacement pages for updating, at no additional cost.

Superintendent of Documents
U.S. Government Printing Office
Washington, DC 20402
(202) 275–2051

Export Briefs

Weekly. $50.00/year.

Subject heading: Produce trade—Periodicals

Provides trade leads of overseas buyers of agricultural products needs and the addresses of firms requesting goods. Also available are individual trade leads at $10.00 per commodity per year.

Export Promotion Division
Foreign Agricultural Service
U.S. Department of Agriculture
Room 4945, South Building
Washington, DC 20250
(202) 447–3448

Export Control Regulations see **The Export Administration Regulations.**

Export Directory

Free.

Subject heading: Export marketing—Directories

Furnishes up-to-date listings and information of interest to firms engaged in exporting.

Foreign Agricultural Service
U.S. Department of Agriculture
Washington, DC 20250
(202) 447-2791

Export Management Companies

1981. 192p. $7.00.

Subject heading: Export marketing

More than 1,100 export-management companies are alphabetically listed and arranged in sections by states. Also included is a supplementary product index of thirty-six basic product/service categories.

Superintendent of Documents
U.S. Government Printing Office
Washington, DC 20402
(202) 275-2051

Export Marketing for Smaller Firms

1979. 4th ed. 90p. $4.75.

Subject heading: Export marketing

Library of Congress Call Number: HF1456 1979 .I57

Describes pertinent information that small firms need to consider when deciding whether to export to expand their sales and profits.

Superintendent of Documents
U.S. Government Printing Office
Washington, DC 20402
(202) 275-2051

FAS Release: Weekly Roundup of World Product and Trade see **FAS Report: Weekly Roundup of World Production and Trade.**

FAS Report: Weekly Roundup of World Production and Trade

Weekly. Free to U.S. residents.

Subject heading: Agriculture—Economic aspects—Periodicals
U.S. Department of Agriculture
Foreign Agricultural Service
Washington, DC 20250
(202) 275–2051

Food and Agricultural Export Directory see **Export Directory.**

Foreign Agricultural Trade of the United States
Bimonthly. $19.00.
Subject heading: Produce trade—United States—Statistics—Periodicals
Library of Congress Call Number: HD9001 .U654

Furnishes information concerning imports and exports of agricultural products into and out of the United States.
United States Department of Agriculture
Washington, DC 20250
(202) 447–2791

Foreign Agricultural Trade of the United States Digest see **Foreign Agricultural Trade of the United States.**
Foreign Agriculture Trade of the United States, Statistical Report see **Foreign Agricultural Trade of the United States.**

Foreign Business Practices; Materials on Practical Aspects of Exporting, International Licensing and Investing
1981. 124p. $5.50.
Subject heading: Commercial law
Library of Congress Call Number: K1005.4 .U53 1981

Provides useful information concerning foreign business operations. Covers topics such as the use of foreign distributors and agents; treaties and laws protecting patents and trademarks in foreign countries; foreign licensing and joint-venture arrangements; Domestic International Sales Corporation tax benefits; and export trade associations.
Superintendent of Documents
U.S. Government Printing Office
Washington, DC 20402
(202) 275–2051

Foreign Consular Offices in the United States
1982. rev. ed. 223p. Annual. $7.50.
Subject heading: Diplomatic and consular service in the United States—

Registers
Library of Congress Call Number: JX1705 .A28

Furnishes a complete and official list of foreign consular offices in the United States and their jurisdictions and recognized consular offices.
Superintendent of Documents
U.S. Government Printing Office
Washington, DC 20402
(202) 275–2051

Foreign Economic Trends and Their Implications for the United States

$55.00/year.
Individual copies
$1.50.

Subject heading: Economic History—1945–
Library of Congress Call Number: HC10 .E416

Series of brief reports on more than a hundred countries that are prepared by U.S. embassies and consulates, provides current data on gross national product, foreign trade, unemployment figures, wage-and-price index, and so on.
Superintendent of Documents
U.S. Government Printing Office
Washington, DC 20402
(202) 275–2051

Global Market Surveys

Prices vary.

Extensive reports on twenty to thirty of the prime foreign markets for a single U.S. industry or group of industries. Industries studied in these surveys include biomedical equipment, computer equipment, food processing, electronic components, and numerous others.
Superintendent of Documents
U.S. Government Printing Office
Washington, DC 20402
(202) 275–2051

A Guide to Financing Exports
United States Department of Commerce, International Trade Administration.
1980. 20p.
Subject heading: Export credit—United States—Handbooks, manuals, etc.

Contains a listing of U.S. government agencies that will assist in finding buyers for products and also will aid, in cooperation with commercial banks, the financing of sales. In addition, it covers methods used to finance exports.
U.S. Department of Commerce
International Trade Administration
Washington, DC 20230
(202) 377–2000

Highlights of United States Export and Import Trade
Monthly. $55.00.
Subject heading: United States—Commerce—Periodicals
Superintendent of Documents
U.S. Government Printing Office
Washington, DC 20402
(202) 275–2051

How to Build an Export Business: An International Marketing Guide for the Minority Owned Firm
Nelson T. Joyner, Jr., and Richard G. Lurie.
1981. 158p. $5.50.
Subject heading: Export Marketing—Handbooks, manuals, etc.
Superintendent of Documents
U.S. Government Printing Office
Washington, DC 20402
(202) 275–2051

Indexes of Living Costs Abroad and Quarters Allowances
United States Department of State.
Quarterly. $6.50/year.
Subject heading: Cost and standard of living

Publication issued by the Bureau of Labor Statistics of the Department of Labor that provides indexes of living costs abroad, quarters allowances, and hardship differentials.
Superintendent of Documents
U.S. Government Printing Office
Washington, DC 20402
(202) 275–2051

International Commerce see **Business America.**

International Economic Indicators see **International Economic Indicators and Competitive Trends.**

International Economic Indicators and Competitive Trends
Quarterly. $13.00/year.
Subject heading: Economic indicators—Periodicals
Library of Congress Call Number: HC59 .U525a

Contains economic data for the United States and seven principal industrial countries. Included are statistics on gross national product, industrial production, trade, prices, finance, and labor.
Superintendent of Documents
U.S. Government Printing Office
Washington, DC 20402
(202) 275-2051

International Relations Dictionary
1980. 80p. $5.00.
Subject heading: International relations—Dictionaries

Provides terms, phrases, acronyms, catch words, and abbreviations used in international business.
Superintendent of Documents
U.S. Government Printing Office
Washington, DC 20402
(202) 275-2051

Market Share Reports
Annual. $9.00/each.
Subject heading: Commercial products—United States—Periodicals

Provides exporters with information on imports of approximately 1,500 manufactured products from the United States as well as eight leading suppliers into foreign markets. Covers this information for eighty-eight import markets.
National Technical Information Services
U.S. Department of Commerce
Springfield, VA 22161
(202) 377-2000

The National Income and Product Accounts of the United States: Statistical Tables
United States Bureau of Economic Analysis.
1981. 88p. $3.75.
Subject heading: Gross national product—United States—Statistics
Library of Congress Call Number: HC110.I5 A3

Notes: Special supplement to the *Survey of Current Business*

Superintendent of Documents
U.S. Government Printing Office
Washington, DC 20402
(202) 275–2051

Overseas Business Reports

$44.00/year.

Subject heading: Commerce—Collected works
Library of Congress Call Number: HF91 .U482

Provides current and detailed marketing information for businesses evaluating the export market. Includes trade outlooks, statistics, advertising and market research, distribution and sales channels, regulations, and market profiles, and so on. The one hundred plus countries include Pakistan, Netherlands, Colombia, Bahrain, Kenya, Ecuador, Cyprus, and Argentina. Also contains economic and commercial profiles of the various countries.
Superintendent of Documents
U.S. Government Printing Office
Washington, DC 20402
(202) 275–2051

Profiles of Labor Conditions see **Country Labor Profiles.**

Recent Commerce Department Publications see **Commerce Publications Update.**

Small Business Market Is the World

Free.

Programs designed to assist small-business entry into or expansion in international markets are described.
U.S. Small Business Administration
Office of International Trade
1441 L Street, N.W.
Washington, DC 20416
(202) 653–6565

Survey of Current Business

Monthly. $50.00.

Subject heading: Business—Periodicals
Library of Congress Call Number: HC101 .A13

Provides statistical information on business, national income and product, foreign and domestic investments, and trade.

Superintendent of Documents
U.S. Government Printing Office
Washington, DC 20402
(202) 275–2051

Tariff Schedules of the United States
1982. Loose leaf. $32.00.
Subject heading: Tariff-law and legislation—United States

Contains the legal text of the amended and modified versions of the Tariff Schedules of the United States, along with annotations defining statistical information for customs forms.
Superintendent of Documents
U.S. Government Printing Office
Washington, DC 20402
(202) 275–2051

United States Department of Commerce Publications Catalog, 1980
1981. 306p. $8.50.

This catalog contains listings of Department of Commerce entries in the 1980 GPO monthly catalogs.
Superintendent of Documents
U.S. Government Printing Office
Washington, DC 20402
(202) 275–2051

U.S. Department of State Indexes of Living Costs Abroad and Quarters Allowance see **Indexes of Living Costs Abroad and Quarters Allowances.**

U.S. Export Management Companies: Directory
1981. 192p. $7.00.
Subject heading: Export associations—United States—Directories

Provides a listing of more than 1,100 export management companies arranged in sections by states. Also contains a product index of thirty-six basic production/service categories.
U.S. Department of Commerce
International Trade Administration
Washington, DC 20230
(202) 377–2000

U.S. Foreign Trade: Highlights of Exports and Imports see **Highlights of U.S. Exports and Imports.**

1982 U.S. Industrial Outlook: for 200 Industries with Projections for 1986

$10.00.

Subject heading: United States—Industries—Periodicals
Library of Congress Call Number: HC101 .U54

Contains up-to-date data and forecasts to 1986 for more than two hundred industries. Objective analyses of each industry are provided by the staff of the Bureau of Industrial Economics.
Superintendent of Documents
U.S. Government Printing Office
Washington, DC 20402
(202) 275–2051

World Agriculture Outlook & Situation

3 per year.

Subject heading: Agriculture—Statistics—Periodicals
Division of Information
Office of Management Services
U.S. Department of Agriculture
Washington, DC 20250
(202) 447–2791

World Agricultural Situation see **World Agriculture Outlook & Situation.**

World Agricultural Supply and Demand Estimates

Monthly with 4 additional issues per year. $30.00.

Subject heading: Farm produce—United States—Periodicals
Library of Congress Call Number: HD9001 .U55b

Mainly composed of tables and statistics. Also provides news items on forecasted supply or demand of agricultural commodities.
U.S. Department of Agriculture
Room 0054
South Building
Washington, DC 20250
(202) 447–2791

World Electric Current Characteristics see **Electric Current Abroad.**

2 Subscriptions and Continuations (Journals, Annuals, Loose-Leaf Services)

Accelerated Development in Sub-Saharan Africa: An Agenda for Action

1981. 206p. Free.
Subject heading: Africa, Sub-Saharan—Economic Conditions—1960–
Library of Congress Call Number: HC800 .A54

Discusses factors explaining the slow economic growth in Africa's recent past, analyzes policy changes and programs needed to promote growth, and outlines recommendations to donors. The plan for action includes policy and program directions, overall priorities for action, and key areas for donor attention.

World Bank Headquarters
1818 H Street, N.W.
Washington, DC 20433
(202) 477–1234

Across the Board

Monthly. $30.00.
Subject heading: United States—Economic conditions—1971– — Periodicals
Library of Congress Call Number: HC101 .C64

Formerly *The Conference Board Record.* Contains information of current and future interest to managers in business and industry.

The Conference Board, Inc.
845 Third Avenue
New York, NY 10022
(212) 759–0900

The Activities of GATT

Annual. $8.00.
Subject heading: Tariff
Library of Congress Call Number: HF1721 .C55

Gives a brief record of GATT activities for the year covered.

UNIPUB
1180 Avenue of the Americas
New York, NY 10036
(212) 764–2791

Advertising Age

Weekly. $50.00/year.

Subject heading: Advertising—Periodicals
Library of Congress Call Number: HF5801 .A276
Crain Communications, Inc.
740 Rush Street
Chicago, IL 60611
(312) 649–5200

Advertising Age Europe see **Advertising Age's Focus: The European Journal of Advertising and Marketing.**

Advertising Agency Magazine see **Advertising Age.**

Advertising Age's Focus: The European Journal of Advertising and Marketing

11 monthly issues. $35.00/year.

Subject heading: Advertising—Europe—Periodicals
Library of Congress Call Number: HF5801 .A293
Advertising Age
740 Rush Street
Chicago, IL 60611
(312) 649–5200

Advertising World

Bimonthly. $30.00.

Subject heading: Advertising—Periodicals
Directories International, Inc.
Suite 610
150 Fifth Avenue
New York, NY 10011
(212) 807–1660

American Export Register

1982. Annual. 2 vols. $95.00.

Subject heading: United States—Commerce—Directories
Library of Congress Call Number: HF3010 .A6

Contains a listing of 38,000 American manufacturers offering products for sale overseas. Included under each listing are the company's name, address, telephone, telex and TWX numbers, cable address, export sales and advertising executive, market areas served, and products sold.

Thomas International Publishing Company, Inc.
One Penn Plaza
New York, NY 10119
Attention: Virginia M. Lott, Circulation Manager
(212) 695–0500

American Import Export Bulletin see **American Import Export Management.**

American Import Export Management

Monthly. $25.00.
Subject heading: United States—Commerce—Periodicals
Library of Congress Call Number: HF1 .A58

Contains laws, rulings, articles, news, and trade opportunities.
North American Publishing Company
401 North Broad Street
Philadelphia, PA 19108
(215) 574–9600

American Register of Exporters and Importers see **American Export Register**

American Shipper

Monthly. $15.00.
Subject heading: Shipping—United States—Periodicals
Howard Publications, Inc.
33 South Hogan Street
Post Office Box 4728
Jacksonville, FL 32201
(904) 355–2601

Annalist see **Business Week.**

Announcements of Foreign Investment in U.S. Manufacturing Industries

Quarterly.
Subject heading: Investments, Foreign—United States—Periodicals

Lists announcements of foreign direct investments. Classified by state and industry.

The Conference Board, Inc.
845 Third Avenue
New York, NY 10022
(212) 759–0900

Annual International Congress Calendar see **International Publications Services.**

Annual Report on Exchange Arrangements and Exchange Restrictions

Annual. First copy free; each additional, $12.00.

Subject heading: Foreign Exchange—Law
Library of Congress Call Number: K4440.A13 I57

Examines exchange controls and restrictions with direct implications for the balance of payments of member countries.
International Monetary Fund
Publications Unit, Room C-200
700 19th Street, N.W.
Washington, DC 20431
(202) 477–2945

Annual Report on Exchange Restrictions see **Annual Report on Exchange Arrangements and Exchange Restrictions.**

Asian Wall Street Journal

Weekly. $96.00/year.

Dow Jones & Company, Inc.
22 Cortland Street
New York, NY 10007
(212) 285–5000

BI/Data Printout Summary see **Worldwide Economic Indicators.**

Balance of Payments: Global Data

1980. Quarterly. $21.80 including airmail.

Provides six-year global balance-of-payments data for United States, Japan, and each Economic Community member state. *Balance of Payments: Geographical Breakdown* is a comparison volume that gives a regional breakdown of these figures for a five-year period.

European Community Information Service
Suite 707
2100 M Street, N.W.
Washington, DC 20037
(202) 862–9500

Balance of Payments Statistics
Monthly, plus yearbook. $33.00/year.
Subject heading: Balance of Trade—Yearbooks

Contains monthly issues and a two-part yearbook consisting of balance-of-payments statistics of over 110 countries.
International Monetary Fund
Publications Unit, Room C-200
700 19th Street, N.W.
Washington, DC 20431
(202) 477–2945

Balance of Payments Yearbook see **Balance of Payments Statistics.**

Banks
Most banks collect credit information on foreign firms from correspondent banks overseas. Customers can often obtain this information free of charge or for a small fee.

Bottin International: International Business Register 1982
1982. 185th ed. Annual. 2 vols. $117.50.
Subject heading: Commerce—Directories
Library of Congress Call Number: HF54.F8 B6

Worldwide classified directory, listing over 300,000 manufacturers, producers, exporters, importers, and traders in 151 countries. Also includes names of banks, hotels, and so on.
International Publications Service
114 East 32nd Street
New York, NY 10016
(212) 685–9351

British Journal of Marketing see **European Journal of Marketing.**

Brookings Papers on Economic Activity
3 times a year. $20.00.

Subject heading: United States—Economic Conditions—1961–Periodicals
Library of Congress Call Number: HC101 .B785

Brookings Publications Sales Office
1775 Massachusetts Avenue, N.W.
Washington, DC 20036
(202) 797–6258

Business Horizons

Bimonthly. $15.00.

Subject heading: Business—Periodicals
Library of Congress Call Number: HF5001 .B828

Business Horizons
Graduate School of Business
Indiana University
Bloomington, IN 47405

Business International

Business International provides many publications on international business topics. More information can be obtained by writing to Business International Corporation. Some examples of what they provide are listed below:

Business International: A weekly publication containing current information in international management, marketing, finance, licensing, exporting, taxation, law, and so on ($520.00/year).

Weekly publications on management information for executives doing business in Europe, Latin America, Asia, China, and Eastern Europe (Price varies).

Profits Under Pressure: Studies the European business climate and analyzes how companies are dealing with it ($235.00/year).

Business Strategies for the People's Republic of China: Gives the businessman information on entering the Chinese market, whom to contact, examples of Chinese import and export contracts, exhibit information, advertising, negotiating, and so on ($255.00).

Trading in Latin America—The Impact of Changing Policies: Contains new trade rules for this area and provides a look at the constantly changing import and export rules ($280.00).

Strategic Planning for International Corporations: Organization, Systems, Issues & Trends: Contains information on current concerns of corporate planners and hints on how to cope with them ($180.00).

For more information contact:
Business International Corporation
One Dag Hammarskjold Plaza
New York, NY 10017
(212) 750–6300

Business International Weekly Reports

$520.00/year.

Contains current information and sales-generating ideas, analysis, and actual corporate experience.
Business International Corporation
One Dag Hammarskjold Plaza
New York, NY 10017
(212) 750–6300

Business Strategies for the People's Republic of China see **Business International.**

Business Week

Weekly. $34.95.
Subject heading: Business—Periodicals
Library of Congress Call Number: HF5001 .B89

McGraw-Hill Publications Company
1221 Avenue of the Americas
New York, NY 10020
(212) 997–1221

CA Magazine

Monthly. $20.00.
Subject heading: Accounting—Periodicals
Library of Congress Call Number: HF5601 .C3

Canadian Institute of Chartered Accountants
250 Bloor Street, E.
Toronto, Ontario M4W 1G5
Canada

CCH Topical Law Reports

Price varies.
Subject heading: Accountants—Legal status, Laws, etc.—United States

New business law and tax developments are compiled including domestic

and foreign labor law, social security, banking, securities. Some titles included in this series are: *British Tax Guide*, *Common Market Reports*, *Euromarket News*, and *Income Taxes Worldwide*.
Commerce Clearing House, Inc.
4025 West Peterson Avenue
Chicago, IL 60646
(312) 583–8500

Canadian Business
Monthly. $21.00.
Subject heading: Canada—Commerce—Periodicals
Canadian Business
70 The Esplanade
Toronto, Ontario M5E IR2
Canada

Canadian Business Review
Quarterly. $15.00.
Subject heading: Canada—Economic conditions, 1945– — Periodicals
Library of Congress Call Number: HC111 .C1916

The Canadian Business Review
Suite 100
25 McArthur Road
Ottawa, Ontario,
Canada

Capital Formation and Investment Incentives Around the World
Walter H. Diamond and Dorothy B. Diamond
Loose leaf $120.00.
Subject heading: Investments, Foreign—Law and legislation
Library of Congress Call Number: K3830.4 .D5

Includes in-depth examinations of forty-three countries covering the advantages and disadvantages of a subsidiary corporation vs. a foreign branch, how to incorporate successfully, capital requirements for corporations, tax rebates, tax credits, and so on.
Matthew Bender
DM Department
1275 Broadway
Albany, NY 12201
(518) 465–3575
(800) 833–3630

China Directory see **International Publications Service.**

Clipper Cargo Horizons see **Worldwide Marketing Horizons.**

Columbia Journal of World Business

$32.00.

Subject heading: Business—Periodicals
Library of Congress Call Number: HF5001 .C64

Articles in this journal cover such topics as foreign investments, international economics, financing international business, and international marketing and management.
Columbia University
Trustees of Columbia University
408 Uris
New York, NY 10027
(212) 280–1754

Commerce of the Nation see **Canadian Business.**

Commodity Year Book
1982. Annual. $32.95.
Subject heading: Commercial products—Periodicals
Library of Congress Call Number: HF1041 .C56

Contains such information needed for making decisions in futures market as interest rates of 110 basic commodities, over 85 long-range price charts, and over 830 current key supply/demand statistical tables.
Commodity Research Bureau
One Liberty Plaza
New York, NY 10006
(212) 267–3600

Commodity Year Book: Statistical Abstract Service
3 times a year. $45.00/year.
Subject heading: Commercial products—Periodicals

Updates the information in the *Commodity Year Book.*
Commodity Research Bureau
One Liberty Plaza
New York, NY 10006
(212) 267–3600

Common Market Reporter

Every 2 weeks. Loose leaf for updating. $860.00/year.

Subject heading: European Economic Community
Library of Congress Call Number: HC241.2 .C6

Commerce Clearing House
4025 West Peterson Avenue
Chicago, IL 60646
(312) 583–8500

Conference Board Record see **Across the Board.**

Consumer Europe 1982

1982. 716p. $180.00.

Subject heading: Consumption (Economics)—Europe—Periodicals
Library of Congress Call Number: HD7022 .C68

Handbook of European consumer behavior, focusing on Western Europe. Countries covered include: Austria, Belgium, Denmark, Finland, France, Germany, Great Britain, Italy, Netherlands, Norway, Spain, Sweden, and Switzerland. Gives data on the production, distribution, sales, and other aspects of more than 150 consumer-product categories.
Gale Research Company
Book Tower
Detroit, MI 48226
(313) 961–2242

Container News

Monthly. $21.00/year.

Subject heading: Containerization—Periodicals
Library of Congress Call Number: TA1215 .C5934

Discusses new products and innovations in domestic and international intermodalism.
Container News
Attention: Circulation Department
6285 Barfield Road
Atlanta. GA 30328
(404) 256–9800

Continental Europe Market Guide

1982. Semiannual. 2 vols. $170.00.

Subject heading: Europe—Industries—Directories
Library of Congress Call Number: HC240 .D8

Contains facts on marketing, traffic, sales, purchasing, and credit needed to successfully do business in nineteen countries in continental Europe. Other Dun and Bradstreet international publications on Argentina, Australia, Brazil, Canada, Ireland, Israel, Puerto Rico, Rhodesia, South Africa, United Kingdom, and the world are also available.
Dun and Bradstreet International
Credit Services Offices
Suite 9069
One World Trade Center
New York, NY 10048
(212) 285–7000

Controller see **Financial Executive.**

Corporate Plans and Projects
Quarterly.
Subject heading: Corporations—Periodicals

Provides classifications by state and industry of announced new plant locations in the United States by foreign and domestic companies.
The Conference Board, Inc.
845 Third Avenue
New York, NY 10022
(212) 759–0900

Corporate Publications and Annual Reports
One of the best sources of information about a company's operations are the company's own publications. These publications provide information on the company and industry activity in international business.

Annual reports, the basic reporting documents, disclose a wealth of information concerning the operations of the company. These reports are published by U.S.-based companies and an increasing number of non-U.S.-based multinational corporations.

In addition, from time to time most larger companies publish selected documents describing various aspects of their operations. These documents often provide a valuable summary of the company's international activity.

House organs are a third source of company information. Although they are usually circulated only internally, copies and programs can often be obtained.

Croner Publications, Inc.
Croner Publications, Inc., publishes a variety of sources of interest to the international businessman. Among these are their Kompass publications

on Australia, Belgium, Denmark, France, Holland, Indonesia, Italy, Morocco, Norway, Singapore, Spain, Sweden, Switzerland, the United Kingdom, and West Germany. In addition, some other titles include the *American Export Register*, *Australian Importers*, *Canadian Trade Index*, *Directory of British Importers*, and *Major Companies of the Arab World*.

For more information contact:
Croner Publications, Inc.
211-03 Jamaica Avenue
Queens Village, NY 11428
(212) 464–0866

Croner's Reference Book for Exporters see **Croner's Reference Book for World Traders.**

Croner's Reference Book for World Traders

Monthly updates.
1981 ed. 3 vols. $85.00/year.
Subject heading: Commercial law

Volume 1 provides the basic rules of exporting, a guide to import-tariff systems in foreign countries, foreign import-and-exchange controls, and so on. Volumes 2 and 3 provide general information on all foreign countries including consulates, embassies, hotels, advertising agencies, banks, and freight forwarders.
Croner Publications, Inc.
211-03 Jamaica Avenue
Queens Village, NY 11428
(212) 464–0866

Croner's World Register of Trade Directories see **Trade Directories of the World.**

Currency Profiles

$930.00/year.

Manufacturers Hanover Trust Company
Foreign Exchange Advisory Service
350 Park Avenue
New York, NY 10022
(212) 350–3300

Development Forum

Biweekly. $250.00/year.
Subject heading: Economic development—Periodicals
Library of Congress Call Number: HC59 .D46

Lists announcements of tenders for the World Bank, the Inter-American Development Bank, Asian Development Bank, and Commission of European Communities. Also provides articles on development matters and economic profiles, with an important section on guides to new projects. In addition, the subscription includes the World Bank's *Monthly Operational Summary*.
Development Forum Business Edition
Subscriptions Department
United Nations
CH-1211 Geneva 10
Switzerland

Direction of Trade Statistics
12 monthly issues and yearbook. $30.00/year.
Subject heading: Commerce—Statistics—Periodicals
Library of Congress Call Number: HF91 .I652

Includes export and import data on 135 countries.
International Monetary Fund
Publications Unit, Room C-200
700 19th Street, N.W.
Washington, DC 20431
(202) 477–2945

Directory of Corporate Affiliation
1983. Annual (includes 5 updating bulletins).
Subject heading: Commerce—United States—Directories

Presents an in-depth opinion of major U.S. corporations and their division subsidiaries and affiliates.
National Register Publishing Company
5201 Old Orchard Road
Skokie, IL 60017
(312) 470–3100

Direction of Trade (Monthly) see **Direction of Trade Statistics.**

Doing Business in [country] see **Price Waterhouse Guide Series.**

Doing Business in Europe
Base volume plus monthly loose-leaf updates. $375.00.
Subject heading: Commercial law—European Community Countries

Commerce Clearing House, Inc.
4025 West Peterson Avenue
Chicago, IL 60646
(312) 583–8500
Note: Includes *Euromarket News*

Doing Business With Eastern Europe

10 base volumes plus monthly loose-leaf updates. $18.50.

Subject heading: Europe, Eastern—Commerce—Handbooks, manuals, etc.
Business International Corporation
One Dag Hammarskjold Plaza
New York, NY 10017
(212) 750–6300

The Dow Jones-Irwin Business and Investment Almanac

Edited by Sumner N. Levine.
1982. Annual. $19.95.
Subject heading: Business—Periodicals
Library of Congress Call Number: HF5003 .D68a

Provides coverage of real estate, mutual funds, stock options, gold, futures, fixed-income securities. Also contains a section on foreign interest rates.
Dow Jones-Irwin Business Books
1818 Ridge Road
Homewood, IL 60430
(312) 798–6000

Dow Jones-Irwin Business Almanac see **The Dow Jones-Irwin Business and Investment Almanac.**

Dun & Bradstreet Middle Market Directory see **Million Dollar Directory.**

EFTA Bulletin

Monthly.
Subject heading: European Free Trade Association—Periodicals
Library of Congress Call Number: HF1531 .E2

European Free Trade Association
Press and Information Service
9–11 Rue de Varembe, CH-1211
Geneva 20 Switzerland

E.I.U. Special Reports see **The Economist Intelligence Unit.**

Economic Development and Cultural Change
Quarterly. $50.00.
Subject heading: Economic Policy—Periodicals
Library of Congress Call Number: HC10 .C453

Economic Development and Cultural Change
The University of Chicago Press
5801 Ellis Avenue
Chicago, IL 60637
(312) 753–3331

Economic Handbook of the World
1981. Annual. 608p. $39.95.
Subject heading: Economic History, 1971– —Handbooks, manuals, etc.
McGraw-Hill Book Company
1221 Avenue of the Americas
New York, NY 10020
(212) 997–1221

Economics Selections: An International Bibliography
2 vols. per year. $75.00.
Subject heading: Economics—Bibliography

An annotated bibliography of publications on economics, business, and finance. There is also a section devoted specifically to international economics.
Gordon Breach, Science Publishers, Inc.
One Park Avenue
New York, NY 10016
(212) 689–0360

Economist
Weekly. $75.00.
Subject heading: Economic history—Periodicals
Library of Congress Call Number: HC11 .E2

Economist Newspaper Ltd.
25 Saint James Street
London SWIA 1HG England

The Economist Intelligence Unit
There are many publications distributed by The Economist Intelligence Unit that are important to the international business manager. A few are

listed here in order to give the reader a starting point on finding more in-depth information.

Quarterly Economic Reviews: Eighty-three separate reviews that cover more than 160 countries. These reports evaluate growth prospects, assess opportunities, and analyze the latest economic indicators. There is also an annual supplement for each review including statistical tables on economic indicators over a long-term as well as current economic structure. Rates vary depending on number of reviews purchased. Annual subscription to one review (four issues and annual supplement) is $88.00. Annual cost for all eighty-three reviews is $4,668.00.

Multi-Client Studies: This publication provides detailed reports on current market data, objective analysis, forecasts, and competitor information. Some industries and products covered include coal, household-cleaning products, office furniture, video products, mail-order, health foods, and so on. Prices vary.

E.I.U. Special Reports: Each of these special reports covers a single major topic, analyzing each topic in great depth. Some of the titles in this series include: *Motor Vehicle Safety Standards and Product Liability in Japan*; *World Steel: Structure and Prospects in the 1980s*; *The Major European Economies 1982–87*; *The Oil Imports of Developing Countries: Forecasts to 1995*; *Japanese Industry: How to Compete and How to Cooperate*; *World Timber to the Year 2000*; and *Saudi Arabia: The Development Dilemma*. Prices vary. Several other titles available from The Economist Intelligence Unit are:

Multinational Business: A guide to all aspects of multinational corporate enterprises ($210.00/year).

European Trends: Covers the development of EEC and its internal and external political and economic relations ($130.00/year).

Marketing in Europe: Provides a detailed study of consumer markets with emphasis on the original six EEC member countries ($380.00/year).

For more information contact:
The Economist Intelligence Unit
75 Rockefeller Plaza
New York, NY 10019
(212) 541–5730

Enterprise and Development

Monthly. $100.00/year.

Reports on a variety of information sources, including meetings, speeches, interviews, and corporate country programs relating to private-sector investment. Also included are reports on publications by corporations and research groups.
U.S. Council for International Business
1212 Avenue of the Americas
New York, NY 10036
(212) 354–4480

Etranger see **Bottin International: International Business Register 1982.**

Euromarket News see **Doing Business in Europe.**

Euromoney
Monthly. $89.00.
Subject heading: International finance—Periodicals
Library of Congress Call Number: HG3881 .E665

Euromoney Publications, Ltd.
Nestor House
Playhouse Yard
London EC4V 5EX England

Europa Year Book
1982. Annual. 2 vols. $195.00.
Subject heading: Political science—Yearbooks

An international encyclopedia covering recent history, basic economic statistics, constitution, government, political information, newspapers, periodicals, banks, trade and industrial organizations, railroads, educational institutions, and so on for Europe, Afghanistan-Brazil, British Dependent Territories-Zambia.
UNIPUB
1180 Avenue of the Americas
New York, NY 10036
(212) 764–2791

The Europa Yearbook 1982: A World Survey
1982. 23rd ed. $195.00.

Furnishes information concerning recent history, the economy, education, social welfare, communications, government conditions, and so on for each country in the world.

International Publication Service
114 East 32nd Street
New York, NY 10016
(212) 685–9351

Europe: Magazine of the European Community
Bimonthly. $9.00/year.
Subject heading: Steel industry and trade—European Economic Community Countries—Periodicals
Delegation of the Commission of the European Communities
Suite 707
2100 M Street, N.W.
Washington, DC 20037
(202) 862–9500

Europe Community see **Europe: Magazine of the European Community**

European Community see **Europe: Magazine of the European Community.**

European Community Information Service
The European Community Information Service issues a number of publications helpful in international business planning. Some of the many topics covered in these publications include: political and institutional information, customs, agriculture, forestry, fisheries, law, social conditions, transportation, taxation, economic conditions, energy, industry, environment, educational policy, statistics, and so on. While there are many titles available in all the preceding areas, some of their more general publications are listed below:
External Trade Bulletin ($90.00/year, monthly).

Balance of Payments: Global Data ($31.80/year, quarterly).

Official Journal of the European Communities ($600.00/year, daily).

Agricultural Markets: Prices ($103.00, 10 issues plus 2 supplements).

Bulletin of the European Communities ($69.75, 11 issues and index).

For more information contact:
European Community Information Service
Suite 707
2100 M Street, N.W.
Washington, DC 20037
(202) 862–9500

1982–1986 European Forecasting Study

Twice a year. $225.00/one country; $1,450.00/full 16-country study.

Sixteen countries included in the study are: Austria, Belgium, Denmark, Finland, France, Germany, Greece, Ireland, Italy, Netherlands, Norway, Portugal, Spain, Sweden, Switzerland, and the United Kingdom.
Business International Corporation
One Dag Hammarskjold Plaza
New York, NY 10017
(212) 750–6300

European Journal of Marketing

7 times a year. $197.95.

Subject heading: Marketing—Periodicals

A British journal providing articles on all aspects of world marketing policies and practices.
MCB Publications, Ltd.
198-200 Keighley Road
Bradford BD9 4JQ
West Yorkshire England

The European Parliament

Irregular. Free.

European Communities
Suite 707
2100 M Street, N.W.
Washington, DC 20037
(202) 862–9500

European Trends

Quarterly. $148.00/year including airmail.

Subject heading: European Economic Community—Periodicals
Library of Congress Call Number: HC241.2 .E87

Analyzes European developments and covers the developments of the EEC, its internal and external political, legal, and economic relations
The Economist Intelligence Unit
75 Rockefeller Plaza
New York, NY 10019
(212) 541–5730

Eurostatistics

Monthly. $42.75. Includes airmail.

Subject heading: European Economic Community Countries—Economic conditions—Statistics—Periodicals

Library of Congress Call Number: HC241.2.A1 S57a

European Community Information Service
Suite 707
2100 M Street, N.W.
Washington, DC 20037
(202) 862–9500

Executive Living Costs in Major Cities Worldwide 1982

Annual. $4,165.00 (for 85 cities). Can be purchased separately.

Business International Corporation
World Headquarters
One Dag Hammarskjold Plaza
New York, NY 10017
(212) 750–6300

EXIMBANK Intelligence Weekly

Weekly, plus 4 quarterly indexes. $195.00/year.

Covers export/import and international investment guarantees.

R&H Publishers
Box 3587 Georgetown Post Office
Washington, DC 20007

EXIMBANK Program Summary

Free.

Summarizes the various programs through which Eximbank cooperates with the private sector. Also provides information on export financing.

Export-Import Bank of the United States
Room 1167
811 Vermont Avenue, N.W.
Washington, DC 20571
(202) 566–8990

Export

Bimonthly. $40.00.

Contains information of interest to distributors and dealers of consumer hardgoods overseas.
Sales Manager
Johnston International
386 Park Avenue, S.
New York, NY 10016

Export Directory/U.S. Buying Guide
Biennial. $175.00.
Subject heading: United States—Commerce—Directories
Journal of Commerce
110 Wall Street
New York, NY 10005
(212) 425–1616

Export Shipping Manual
Weekly. Loose leaf for updating. $245.00.
The Bureau of National Affairs, Inc.
1231 25th Street, N.W.
Washington, DC 20037
(202) 452–4200

Exporters Directory/U.S. Buying Guide
1983–1984. 2 vols. $225.00.
Subject heading: United States—Commerce—Directories
The Journal of Commerce
445 Marshall Street
Phillipsburg, NJ 08865
(201) 859–1300
Note: Supplemented by *Foreign Markets for Your Products.*

F & S Index Europe
Monthly, with quarterly cumulations; also in annual cumulation. $540.00.
Subject heading: Europe—Industries—Periodicals—Indexes
Predicasts
11001 Cedar Avenue
Cleveland, OH 44106
(800) 321–6388
(216) 795–3000

F & S Index International

Monthly with annual cumulation. $540.00.

Subject heading: Industry—Periodicals—Indexes
Library of Congress Call Number: Z7164.C81 F13

Predicasts
11001 Cedar Avenue
Cleveland, OH 44106
(800) 321–6388
(216) 795–3000

F & S Index of Corporate Change

Quarterly with annual cumulation. $195.00.

Subject heading: Consolidation and merger of corporations—United States—Indexes—Periodicals

Guide to information on mergers, acquisitions, and other organizational changes affecting corporate identity that are covered in newspapers and periodicals. Composed of three sections, one listing companies by SIC, citing the corporate change involved, and providing the citation to the newspaper or periodical article. One is an alphabetical company index, and the third section contains name changes, new companies, reorganizations, and so on.
Predicasts
11001 Cedar Avenue
Cleveland, OH 44106
(800) 321–6388
(216) 795–3000

Far Eastern Economic Review

Weekly. $260.00.

Subject heading: East Asia—Economic Conditions—Periodicals
Far Eastern Economic Review Ltd.
Box 160
Hong Kong, Hong Kong

Finance and Development

Quarterly. Free.

Subject heading: International Finance—Periodicals
Library of Congress Call Number: HG3881 .F85

Contains short articles on world economic and financial problems.

International Monetary Fund
700 19th Street, N.W.
Washington, DC 20431
(202) 477–7000

Financial Executive

Monthly. $22.00.

Subject heading: Business—Periodicals
Library of Congress Call Number: F5001 .F514

Financial Executives Institute
Circulation Manager
633 Third Avenue
New York, NY 10017
(212) 953–0500

Financial Market Trends

5 times a year. $23.55.

Subject heading: Finance—Periodicals
Library of Congress Call Number: HG136 .F56

Trends and prospects in the international and major domestic financial markets of the OECD areas are assessed. Also included are charts, statistics, and reviews.
O.E.C.D. Publications and Information Center
1750 Pennsylvania Avenue, N.W.
Washington, DC 20006
(202) 724–1857

Financial Times

Daily. $365.00/year.

International edition published in Frankfurt, Germany.
Financial Times
75 Rockefeller Plaza
New York, NY 10019
(212) 489–8300

Financial World

Semimonthly; statistical index quarterly. $33.00.

Subject heading: Finance—Periodicals
Library of Congress Call Number: HG4501 .F5

Macro Communications
150 West 58th Street
New York, NY 10022
(202) 826–4360

Financing Foreign Operations

Loose leaf; updated by monthly supplements. $795.00/year.

Subject heading: Investments, American
Library of Congress Call Number: HG4538 .B813

Current guide to help the businessman find sources of capital and credit in thirty-four major markets.
Business International Corporation
Subscription Department
One Dag Hammarskjold Plaza
New York, NY 10017
(212) 750–6300

Florida Journal of Commerce, American Shipper see **American Shipper.**

Focus see **Across the Board.**

Forecasts of Exchange Rate Movements. Dollar Edition see **Currency Profiles.**

Foreign Markets for Your Products
Subject heading: Export Trade

Information on over 37,000 exporters and more than 2,500 products is contained in this complete marketing guide to the U.S. export industry.
The Journal of Commerce
445 Marshall Street
Phillipsburg, NJ 08865
(201) 859–1300
Note: Supplement to *Exporter's Directory/U.S. Buying Guide.*

Foreign Tax and Trade Briefs
Walter H. Diamond.

Loose leaf. 2 vols.

Subject heading: Taxation—Law

Contains trade information and basic tax facts for the principal nations of the world.

Matthew Bender and Company, Inc.
235 East 45th Street
New York, NY 10017
(212) 661–5050

Fortune

Bimonthly. $36.00.
Subject heading: Business—Periodicals
Library of Congress Call Number: HF5001 .F7

Fortune
541 North Fairbanks Court
Chicago, IL 60611
(312) 329–6800

Fraser's Canadian Trade Directory
1980. 69th ed. 3 vols. $95.00.
Subject heading: Canada—Manufacturers—Directories
International Publications Service
114 East 32nd Street
New York, NY 10016
(212) 685–9351

Fund and Bank Review see **Finance and Development.**

Futures Market Service

Weekly. $110.00/year.
Subject heading: Commodity exchanges—United States—Periodicals

More commonly known as the "blue sheet," this weekly covers factors influencing commodity prices. Current market statistics are included for each commodity actively traded on the futures market. Each issue has calendar of commodity events.
Commodity Research Bureau
One Liberty Plaza
New York, NY 10006
(212) 267–3600

GATT Activities see **The Activities of GATT.**

Global Investment Flows

Quarterly.
Subject heading: Investments—Periodicals

Provides a listing of transnational investment flows and the name of the company investing and the country in which the investment will occur.
The Conference Board, Inc.
845 Third Avenue
New York, NY 10022
(212) 759–0900

Government Finance Statistics Yearbook
1982. Vol. 6 $13.00/volume.
Subject heading: Finance, public—Statistics—Periodicals
Library of Congress Call Number: HJ101 .G68

Provides information on the various units of government, government accounts, the enterprises and financial institutions that governments own and control, and the national sources of data on government operations.
International Monetary Fund
Publications Unit, Room C-200
700 19th Street, N.W.
Washington, DC 20431
(202) 477–2945

Growth of World Industry see **Yearbook of Industrial Statistics.**

Handling and Shipping see **Handling and Shipping Management.**

Handling and Shipping Management
Monthly. $30.00.
Subject heading: Materials handling—Periodicals
Library of Congress Call Number: TS149 .H32

Handling and Shipping Management
Post Office Box 95759
Cleveland, OH 44101

Harvard Business Review
Bimonthly. $21.00.
Subject heading: Business—Periodicals
Library of Congress Call Number: HF5001 .H3

Harvard Business Review
Subscription Service Department
Post Office Box 3000
Woburn, MA 01888

ILO Publications

Quarterly. Free.

ILO Branch Office
1750 New York Avenue, N.W.
Washington, DC 20006
(202) 376–2315

IMF Survey

Semimonthly. $23.00/year.

Subject heading: International finance—Periodicals
Library of Congress Call Number: HG3881 .I6197

Contains information on IMF activities, topical articles, and financial and economic news.
International Monetary Fund
700 19th Street, N.W.
Washington, DC 20431
(202) 477–2945

Importers and Exporters Trade Promotion Guide

1st ed. Biennial. $5.00.

Subject heading: Foreign trade promotion—Directories
Library of Congress Call Number: HF54.U5 I47

World Wide Trade Service
Box 283
Medina, WA 98039

Industrial Equipment News

Free to qualified subscribers in West Europe, East Europe, and the Middle East.

Published eight times a year in Brussels. Contains editorials and advertisements featuring product news from firms in Europe, the United States, Japan, and Brazil and Spanish America. Reaches more than 60,000 key specifying and buying influences in industrial plants employing twenty-five or more people through IEN-Europe's controlled circulation.
Thomas International Publishing Company, Inc.
One Penn Plaza
New York, NY 10119

Industrial Marketing

Monthly. $20.00.

Subject heading: Advertising—Periodicals
Library of Congress Call Number: HF5801 .I45

Industrial Marketing
Circulation Department
740 Rush Street
Chicago, IL 60611
(312) 649–5260

Inter-American Economic Affairs

Quarterly. $25.00.

Subject heading: Central America—Economic conditions—Periodicals; North America—Economic conditions—Periodicals; South America—Economic conditions—Periodicals
Library of Congress Call Number: HC161 .I585

Inter-American Affairs Press
Post Office Box 181
Washington, DC 20044

International Advertiser

Bimonthly. $15.00/year.

Roth International, Inc.
615 West 22nd Street
Oak Brook, IL 60521
(312) 986–0064

International Banking and Finance

Robert D. Fraser.
1st ed. 2 vols. $75.00.
Subject heading: International finance
Library of Congress Call Number: HG3881 .F7117

Covers export/import financing. Companion periodical is *"EXIMBANK" Intelligence Weekly*, which gives the details of international transactions. Contains information that sets the worldwide operational framework for international banking and finance.
R & H Publishers
Box 3587 Georgetown Post Office
Washington, DC 20007

International Bibliography, Information, Documentation

Quarterly.
Subject heading: United Nations—Bibliography
Library of Congress Call Number: Z6482 .I55

Contains an annotated list of the United Nations systems current publications.

R. R. Bowker Co.
1180 Avenue of the Americas
New York, NY 10036
(212) 764-5100

International Business Report

1981. Annual. 352p. $39.50.
Subject heading: Commerce—Periodicals
Library of Congress Call Number: HF1 .I554

Provides information on outgoing foreign investment, regional and country developments, profitability and investment patterns, corporate planning and strategies, antitrust, taxation, and legal affairs. Also contains statistical material that provides charts and graphs in areas such as foreign profit performance by industry, profitability and investment patterns, and indicators of market size.
Praeger Publishers, CBS Educational and Professional Publishers, A Division of CBS, Inc.
521 Fifth Avenue
New York, NY 10175
(212) 599-8400

International Business Review

Monthly. $85.00/year.

Covers Washington-based developments in international business—international economic policy and legislation as it is conceived and developed.
International Division
U.S. Chamber of Commerce
1615 H Street, N.W.
Washington, DC 20062
(202) 659-6000

International Economic Review

3 times per year. $30.00.
Subject heading: Economics—Periodicals
Library of Congress Call Number: HB1 .I65

University of Pennsylvania
Philadelphia, PA 19104

International Economic Scoreboard

Bimonthly.
Subject heading: Economic indicators—Periodicals

Gives information on the leading economic indicators of seven major industrial countries.
The Conference Board
845 Third Avenue
New York, NY 10022
(212) 759–0900

The International Executive
3 times a year. $130.00/year.
Subject heading: Commerce—Abstracts—Periodicals
Library of Congress Call Number: HF1 .I56

The International Executive
Post Office Box 861
White River Junction, VT 05001

International Financial Statistics
Monthly plus 1
yearbook plus
2 supplements. $75.00/year.
Subject heading: Finance—Statistics—Periodicals
Library of Congress Call Number: HG61 .I57

All aspects of international and domestic finance are covered in this standard source of international statistics. Provides current information on international liquidity, money and banking, international trade, prices, production, government finance, interest rates, the analysis of problems of international payments and of inflation and deflation, and so on. Arranged by country.
International Monetary Fund
700 19th Street, N.W.
Washington, DC 20431
(202) 477–2945

International Journal of Management and Organization see **International Studies of Management and Organization.**

International Journal of Public Administration
4 times a year. $60.00.
Subject heading: Public administration—Periodicals
Library of Congress Call Number: JA1.A1 I593

Marcel Dekker Journals
Post Office Box 11305
Church Street Station
New York, NY 10049

International Labor Affairs Report

Bimonthly. $150.00.

Subject heading: Labor policy—Periodicals

Covers international labor issues from the aspect of business-community participation in the International Labor Organization, the International Organisation of Employers, the United Nations, the Organization for Economic Cooperation and Development (OECD), and the European Community (EC). Also provides reports on intergovernmental organizations' and international trade-union movements' growing influence on the international labor/management environment.

U.S. Council for International Business
1212 Avenue of the Americas
New York, NY 10036
(212) 354–4480

International Letter

Bimonthly; loose leaf updates. Free.

Subject heading: Banks and banking, International

Federal Reserve Bank of Chicago
Post Office Box 834
Chicago, IL 60690
(312) 322–5322

International Management

Monthly. £21.

Subject heading: Industrial management—Periodicals

McGraw-Hill House
Shoppenhangers Road
Maidenhead, Berkshire
SL6 2QL England

International Management Digest see **International Management.**

International Market Guide Continental Europe see **Continental Europe Market Guide.**

International Marketing Report see **International Advertiser.**

International Monetary Fund

The International Monetary Fund issues a number of publications on many aspects of international business. Some are listed below.

International Financial Statistics (monthly, $75.00/year).

Balance of Payments Manual ($4.00).

Occasional Papers Series: Studies on several economic and financial subjects. Some titles in this series are: *Trade Policy Developments in Industrial Countries*; *International Capital Markets: Recent Developments and Short-Term Prospects*; *International Capital Markets: Developments and Prospects*; and *Effects of Slowdown in Industrial Countries on Growth in Non-Oil Developing Countries.*

For more information write:
International Monetary Fund
Publications Unit
Room C-200
700 19th Street, N.W.
Washington, DC 20431
(202) 477–2945

International Monetary Fund Staff Papers
3 times a year. $9.00/year.

Contains reports of the IMF on the exchange of information on monetary and financial problems.
International Monetary Fund
700 19th Street, N.W.
Washington, DC 20431
(202) 477–2945

International Monetary Market Year Book
1981. $10.00.
Subject heading: Foreign exchange—Periodicals
Library of Congress Call Number: HG3853.F6 I58

Provides daily futures prices for currencies of eight countries traded in the IMM during the year. Also provides silver, gold, and the U.S. Treasury Bills futures prices.
Chicago Mercantile Exchange
444 West Jackson
Chicago, IL 60606
(312) 648–1000

International Outlook: The Corporate Perspective
1982. Annual. $15.00.
Subject heading: Economic history, 1945– —Periodicals

Library of Congress Call Number: HC10 .B33

The Conference Board, Inc.
845 Third Avenue
New York, NY 10022
(212) 759–0900

International Publications Services

International Publications Services provides the international businessman with many general and statistical publications. Some titles supplied by this organization include:

Lloyd's Maritime Directory: 1982. Annual. $95.00. Includes information on over 34,000 vessels and more than 5,000 shipowners and managers throughout the world with addresses, telephone and telex numbers.

Owen's Trade Directory: Business Travel Guide: 1982. Annual. $75.00. Provides economic information and trade lists, manufacturers, importers, banks, and so on for sixty-five countries in the Middle East and Arabian Gulf, Southeast Asia and the Far East, Africa, the Mediterranean, and the West Indies.

China Directory: 1981. Annual. $85.00. Information on government organization of mainland China with names of officials and posts held, foreign-trade bodies, and so on.

Yearbook of Labor Statistics: 1982. $75.00. This summary of principal statistics relating to labor throughout the world is published by the International Labor Organization (ILO).

Annual International Congress Calendar: 1982. $47.50. Lists more than 3,500 meetings through 1986 giving date, place, address of organizing body, theme, and so on.

For more information contact:
International Publications Services
114 East 32nd Street
New York, NY 10016
(212) 685–9351

International Studies of Management and Organization

Quarterly. $37.00.

Subject heading: Management—Periodicals
Library of Congress Call Number: HD28 .I54

M.E. Sharpe, Inc.
80 Business Park Drive
Armonk, NY 10504
(914) 273–1800

International Tax Journal

Bimonthly. $84.00.

Subject heading: Taxation—Periodicals
Library of Congress Call Number: HJ2240 .I68

Panel Publishers
14 Plaza Road
Greenvale, NY 11548
(516) 484–0006

International Tourism

Quarterly. $173.00, includes airmail.

Subject heading: Tourist trade—Periodicals
Library of Congress Call Number: G155.A1 I552

Provides current data and statistics on significant world trends and presents authoritative studies of regional and national markets.
The Economist Intelligence Unit
75 Rockefeller Plaza
New York, NY 10019
(212) 541–5730

International Trade Opportunities see **World Trade and Business Digest.**

International Trade Reporter's Export Shipping Manual see **Export Shipping Manual.**

International Trade Reporter's U.S. Export Weekly see **U.S. Export Weekly.**

International Trade Statistics see **Yearbook of International Trade Statistics.**

International Withholding Tax Treaty Guide
Walter H. Diamond.

Loose leaf. $100.00.

Subject heading: Taxation—Handbooks, manuals, etc.

Contains guidelines and advice on current withholding tax rates for interest paid on foreign loans. In addition, the author includes information on dividends, royalties, bank deposit interest, technical fees, and so on.
Matthew Bender
DM Department
1275 Broadway
Albany, NY 12201
(518) 465–3575
(800) 833–3630

International Year Book and Statesmen's Who's Who 1982
1982. 30th ed. Annual. $140.00.
Subject heading: Political science—Yearbooks
Library of Congress Call Number: JA51 .I57

Contains a directory of international, regional, and national organizations and recent facts and figures about countries throughout the world.
International Publications Service
114 East 32nd Street
New York, NY 10016
(212) 685–9351

JBR, Journal of Business Research see **Journal of Business Research.**

Japan Register of Merchants, Manufacturers and Shippers see **Standard Trade Index of Japan 1982–83.**

Johnston International
Johnston International Publishing Corporation produces various business publications. Some are available free of charge. Several examples of these publications are:

Modern Asia: The Business Magazine for Southeast Asia

Ejectivo: The Magazine of Latin America

Alam Attijarat: Serving Business and Government in the Middle East

Modern Africa: The Business Magazine for the Industrial World

For further information contact:
Johnston International Publishing Corporation
386 Park Avenue South
New York, NY 10016
(212) 689–0120

Journal of Business Research

Quarterly. $50.00.

Subject heading: Business—Periodicals
Library of Congress Call Number: HF5001 .J14

Elsevier North Holland, Inc.
Fulfillment Department
52 Vanderbilt Avenue
New York, NY 10017
(212) 867–9040

Journal of Commerce

5 times a week. $120.00.

Subject heading: Commerce—Periodicals
Twin Coast Newspapers, Inc.
110 Wall Street
New York, NY 10005
(212) 425–1616

Journal of Common Market Studies

Quarterly. $56.00.

Subject heading: European Economic Community—Periodicals
Basil Blackwell
108 Cowley Road
Oxford OX4 IJF England

Journal of Developing Areas

Quarterly. $20.00.

Journal of Developing Areas
Western Illinois University
900 West Adams Street
Macomb, IL 61455

The Journal of Finance

5 times a year. $35.00.

Subject heading: Finance—Periodicals
Library of Congress Call Number: HG1 .J6

R.G. Hawkins, Executive Secretary-Treasurer
Graduate School of Business
New York University
100 Trinity Place
New York, NY 10006
(212) 285–6000

Journal of International Business Studies

Semiannual. $30.00.

Subject heading: International business enterprises—Periodicals
Graduate School of Management
Rutgers University
92 New Street
Newark, NJ 07102

Kelly's Directory of Manufacturers and Merchants Including Industrial Services see **Kelly's Manufacturers and Merchants Directory 1982.**

Kelly's Manufacturers and Merchants Directory 1983

1982. 96th ed. Annual. $110.00.

Subject heading: Great Britain—Commerce—Directories
Library of Congress Call Number: HF54.G7 K4

Provides information on 90,000 British firms that offer a service to industry.
International Publications Service
114 East 32nd Street
New York, NY 10016
(212) 685–9351

Lloyd's Maritime Directory see **International Publications Service.**

Long Range Planning

Bimonthly. $175.00/year.

Subject heading: Management—Periodicals
Library of Congress Call Number: HD1 .L6

Contains comprehensive information for international businessmen on effective strategy and planning.
Pergamon Press
Maxwell House
Fairview Park
Elmsford, NY 10523
(914) 592–7700

Magazine of Business see **Business Week.**

Management World

Bimonthly. $18.00.

Subject heading: Management—Periodicals
Library of Congress Call Number: HD28 .M413

Management World
Julia Bradley, Circulation Manager
AMS Building
2360 Maryland Road
Willow Grove, PA 19090

Marketing Economics: Key Plants

Biennial. $90.00.

Subject heading: United States—Industries—Directories
Library of Congress Call Number: HC102 .M25

Two-part directory of 40,000 plants with one hundred or more employees. Part 1 consists of a geographic listing by state and country, with the plants arranged by SIC number. Part 2 lists the companies by SIC, and by state and country within each industry.
Marketing Economics Institute, Ltd.
108 West 39th Street
New York, NY 10018
(212) 869–8260

Marketing in Europe

Monthly. $425.00/year including airmail.

Subject heading: Europe—Commerce—Periodicals

Provides detailed studies of consumer markets with emphasis on the original six EEC member countries.
The Economist Intelligence Unit
75 Rockefeller Plaza
New York, NY 10019
(212) 541–5730

Marketing News

Semimonthly. $30.00.

Subject heading: Marketing—Periodicals
Central Services Office of the American Marketing Association
Suite 200
250 South Wacker Drive
Chicago, IL 60606
(312) 648–0536

The Markets of Asia/Pacific

$75.00/volume.

Subject heading: Economic conditions, 1945–

This twelve-volume series provides analytical and statistical research data on Singapore, Malaysia, Thailand, Indonesia, Hong Kong and Macau, Taiwan, South Korea, Australia, New Zealand and the Pacific Islands, Japan, and China. Each volume includes extensive information on conducting market research in these countries.

Facts on File, Inc.
Order Department
460 Park Avenue South
New York, NY 10016
(212) 683–2244

Merchandise Trends see **Retail Business Monthly.**

Middle East Executive Reports

$395.00/year.

Updates legal and business developments in the Middle East.

Middle East Executive Reports
1115 Massachusetts Avenue, N.W., No. 6
Washington, DC 20005
(202) 289–3900

Million Dollar Directory

1982.
Subject heading: United States—Industries—Directories
Library of Congress Call Number: HC102 .D8

Dun & Bradstreet, Inc.
Three Century Drive
Parsippany, NJ 07054
(201) 455–0900
Note: Merged with Dun and Bradstreet, Inc., Dun & Bradstreet Middle Market Directory, to form *Million Dollar Directory*.

Monthly External Trade Bulletin

$90.00/year,
including airmail.

Subject heading: European Economic Community countries—Commerce—Periodicals
Library of Congress Call Number: HF181 .S78

European Community Information Service
Suite 707
2100 M Street, N.W.
Washington, DC 20037
(202) 862–9500

Moody's Industrial Manual: American and Foreign
1982. $650.00.
Subject heading: United States—Industries—Yearbooks
Library of Congress Call Number: HG4961 .M67

Moody's Investor's Service
99 Church Street
New York, NY 10007
(212) 553–0300
Note: Includes *Moody's News Reports.*

Moody's Industrial News Reports see **Moody's Industrial Manual: American and Foreign.**

Moody's International Manual
1982. Annual. $750.00.
Subject heading: Corporations—Finance—Directories
Library of Congress Call Number: HG4009 .M66

Provides key financial and business information on over 3,000 major corporations. Information concerning financial statements, debt, capital, management, company histories, and description of business and properties are included.
Moody's Investors Service
99 Church Street
New York, NY 10007
(212) 553–0300
Note: Kept up to date by *Moody's International News Reports* (biweekly, $350.00/year).

Moody's International News Reports see **Moody's International Manual.**

Multi-Client Studies see **The Economist Intelligence Unit.**

Multinational Business

Quarterly. $228.00. Includes airmail.

Subject heading: International business enterprises—Periodicals
Library of Congress Call Number: HD69.I7 M88

A review of developments in all aspects of multinational corporate enterprise, the world trading environment, relations with governments and current problems.
The Economist Intelligence Unit
75 Rockefeller Plaza
New York, NY 10019
(212) 541–5730

Multinational Executive Travel Companion

1982. Annual. $40.00.
Library of Congress Call Number: G153 .M84

Provides information on travel costs, entertainment, restaurants, hotels, business facilities, protocol, business practices, and holidays and trade fairs in 160 countries.
Multinational Executive Inc.
Harvard Square
Post Office Box 92
Cambridge, MA 02138

Multinational Monitor

Monthly. $20.00.
Subject heading: International business enterprises—Periodicals
Corporate Accountability Research Group
Post Office Box 19312
Washington, DC 20036
(202) 833–3931

National Accounts ESA

1982. Annual. $9.50.
Subject heading: National income—European Economic Community countries—Accounting—Statistics—Periodicals
European Community Information Service
Suite 707
2100 M Street, N.W.
Washington, DC 20037
(202) 862–9500

The OECD Economic Outlook

2 times a year. $21.50.

Subject heading: Economic history, 1945- —Periodicals
Library of Congress Call Number: HC10 .018

OECD Publications and Information Center
Suite 1207
1750 Pennsylvania Avenue, N.W.
Washington, DC 20006
(202) 724–1857

OECD Economic Surveys

Annual. $85.90/year.

Subject heading: Economic conditions, 1945- —Periodicals
Library of Congress Call Number: HC605 .074

Provides a brief discussion of current economic trends and statistics for each member country: Australia, New Zealand, Denmark, France, Austria, Turkey, Norway, Switzerland, Belgium/Luxembourg, Greece, Spain, Canada, Iceland, United States, Germany, Japan, Yugoslavia, Sweden, and Ireland.

OECD Publications and Information Center
Suite 1207
1750 Pennsylvania Avenue, N.W.
Washington, DC 20006
(202) 724–2857

OECD Financial Statistics

Semiannual, bimonthly supplements; 2 vols.
bimonthly supplements. $80.00/year.

Subject heading: Finance—Organization for Economic Cooperation and Development countries—Statistics—Periodicals
Library of Congress Call Number: HG136 .073a

Part 1 gives statistics by country on financial topics that include the structure of saving, investment, and financial transactions, general government finance, long-term securities and interest rates. Part 2 and 3 include "The International Market" and "Comparable Tables."

OECD Publications and Information Center
Suite 1207
1750 Pennsylvania Avenue, N.W.
Washington, DC 20006
(202) 724–1857

The OECD Observer

6 issues a year. $15.85. Includes postage.

Subject heading: Europe—Economic conditions, 1945– —Periodicals

Library of Congress Call Number: HC240.A1 02

OECD Publications and Information Center
Suite 1207
1750 Pennsylvania Avenue, N.W.
Washington, DC 20006
(202) 724–1857

On-Line Data-Base Searching

One of the more recent means of obtaining current and complete bibliographic information is through the use of on-line bibliographic database searching. Through this means of searching, the most current material can be indexed and retrieved in the fastest time possible. Since this means of bibliographic retrieval is relatively new, new data bases are continually being developed. Therefore, while only a few are mentioned here, there are many available, and new ones will be available in the future. This list is only intended to introduce the reader to the different types of services available. A few of the more general indexes are listed below.

ABI/Inform: Abstracts over four hundred publications on all aspects of business management and administration.

Disclosure: Provides extracts of all reports filed with the Securities and Exchange Commission.

Foreign Traders Index: Provides a list of firms in 130 countries that import U.S. goods or that would like to represent U.S. exporters. Compiled by the U.S. Department of Commerce.

Predicasts F&S Indexes: Information on domestic and international companies and products.

U.S. Exports: Supplies export statistics on the private and public sectors of the United States. Prepared by the U.S. Bureau of the Census from Shippers' Export Declarations.

Encyclopedia of Associations: Provides pertinent information on several thousand trade and professional organizations.

PAIS International: Indexes over eight hundred journals and 6,000 publications on public-policy issues.

National Newspaper Index: Complete indexing of *The Christian Science Monitor*, *The New York Times*, and *The Wall Street Journal*.

Operations Research/Management Science

Monthly. Loose leaf. $108.00/year.

Executive Science Institute, Inc.
Post Office Box Drawer M
Whippany, NJ 07981
(201) 887–1233

Organisation for Economic Cooperation and Development

The Organisation for Economic Cooperation and Development publishes information on such topics as financial and fiscal affairs, science and technology, energy, education, industry, and agriculture. Some of their publications are listed below.

World Energy Outlook: Important facts and figures on the world energy situation, that is, forecasts for oil, natural gas, coal, and so on. Includes statistical tables and energy-policy guidelines adopted by the IEA ($45.00).

Labor Force Statistics

Quarterly National Accounts Bulletin

Indicators of Industrial Activity

Main Economic Indicators

National Accounts Statistics

For more information contact:
OECD Publications and Information Center
Suite 1207
1750 Pennsylvania Avenue, N.W.
Washington, DC 20006
(202) 724–1857

Owen's Trade Directory: Business Travel Guide see **International Publications Services**

Pacific Basin Quarterly

Free.

Editor, *Pacific Basin Quarterly*
Publications Office
Pacific Basin Center Foundation
Post Office Box 54607
Los Angeles, CA 90054

Pick's Currency Yearbook
1982. $196.00.
Subject heading: Money—Periodicals
Library of Congress Call Number: HG219 .P5

Provides information on the history, transferability, currency developments, varieties, administration and exchange rates of 112 currencies and information on the Eurocurrency market, gold and its prices and movements in many international trading centers.
Pick Publishing Corporation
21 West Street
New York, NY 10006
(212) 425–0591

Predicasts F&S Index Europe see **F&S Index Europe.**

Predicast F&S Index International see **F&S Index International.**

Price Waterhouse Guide Series
A series of guides on various aspects of doing business in the countries where Price Waterhouse has offices or has business contacts. The guides are based on the latest information available, and they are continuously updated. Topics covered include investments, corporate information, business regulations, accounting, taxes, and so on. The company puts out over seventy-five pamphlets on *Doing Business in* [name of country]. In addition, they produce pamphlets on corporate taxes, *East West Trade*, individual taxes, *U.S. Citizens Abroad*, *U.S. Expatriate Compensation*, to name a few.

For more information contact:
Price Waterhouse and Company
1251 Avenue of the Americas
New York, NY 10020
(212) 489–8900

Principal International Business: The World Marketing Directory
1982. Annual. $425.00.
Subject heading: Commerce—Directories—Periodicals
Library of Congress Call Number: HF54.U5 P74

Complete legal name, parent company, address, cable or telex, sales volume, number of employees, SIC number, description of activities, and chief executives are given for over 51,000 businesses. Also contains a list of businesses by products.

Duns Marketing Service
Three Century Drive
Parsippany, NJ 07054
(201) 455–0900

Profits Under Pressure see **Business International.**

Quarterly Economic Reviews see **The Economist Intelligence Unit.**

Results of the Business Survey Carried Out Among Managements in the Community

Monthly. $82.75. Includes airmail.

Subject heading: European Economic Community countries—Economic conditions—Periodicals
Library of Congress Call Number: HC241.2 .A19

European Community Information Service
Suite 707
2100 M Street, N.W.
Washington, DC 20037
(202) 862–9500

Retail Business Monthly

$330.00. Includes airmail.

Subject heading: Retail trade—Great Britain—Periodicals

Covers the economic aspects of the United Kingdom retail trade, emphasizing the consumer-goods market research, distribution patterns and sales trends.
The Economist Intelligence Unit
75 Rockefeller Plaza
New York, NY 10019
(212) 541–5730

Rubber Trends

Quarterly. $283.00. Includes airmail.

Subject heading: Rubber industry and trade—Periodicals
Library of Congress Call Number: HD9161.A1 R83

An analysis and evaluation of market and industrial trends in natural and synthetic rubber.

The Economist Intelligence Unit
75 Rockefeller Plaza
New York, NY 10019
(212) 541–5730

Standard Trade Index of Japan 1982–83
1982. 26th ed. Annual. $135.00.
Subject heading: Japan—Commerce—Directories

Provides current information on over 8,500 major manufacturers, import-and-export trading firms, banks, and business concerns located in Japan. In addition, more than 28,000 commodities and services, Japanese government agencies, foreign embassies and consultants, and trade organizations located in Japan are listed.
International Publications Service
114 East 32nd Street
New York, NY 10016
(212) 685–9351

Statistics of National Income and Expenditure see **Yearbook of National Accounts Statistics.**

Strategic Planning for International Corporations: Organization, Systems, Issues and Trends see **Business International.**

Tax Free Trade Zones of the World
Walter H. Diamond and Dorothy B. Diamond
2 vols. Loose leaf. $170.00.
Subject heading: Free ports and zones
Library of Congress Call Number: HF1418 .D5

Contains information on free perimeters, free ports, transit zones and free trade zones for 378 areas throughout the world that offer the best tax treatments.
Matthew Bender
DM Department
1275 Broadway
Albany, NY 12201
(518) 465–3575
(800) 833–3630

Tax Havens of the World
Walter H. Diamond and Dorothy B. Diamond
2 vols. Loose leaf. $175.00.

Subject heading: Tax havens

Information on six types of tax havens in forty-three countries.
Matthew Bender
DM Department
1275 Broadway
Albany, NY 12201
(518) 465–3575
(800) 833–3630

Trade and Economic Development
Monthly. $350.00/year.
Energy Developments International Review Service, Inc.
15 Washington Place
New York, NY 10003

Trade and Industry Associations
Trade and industry associations collect a significant amount of data on opportunities in foreign markets. Anyone investigating a particular product should inquire at the appropriate trade association to see whether information on the product of interest has been collected. In addition, trade associations frequently collect comprehensive statistical and narrative material on products and industries in the form of yearbooks, which are usually available to the public.

Trade Directories of the World
Loose leaf. $59.95/year.
Subject heading: Directories—Bibliography

Annotated list of business and trade directories. Data is arranged by continent and by country. Includes frequency of publication, price, number of pages, publisher's address, as well as the nature and scope of the publication. Also, an index to "trades and professions" and a country index is included.
Croner Publications, Inc.
211-03 Jamaica Avenue
Queens Village, NY 11428
(212) 464–0866

Note: Kept up to date by "Amendment Service."

Trading in Latin America: The Impact of Changing Policies see **Business International.**

UN Report

Monthly. $100.00/year.

Reports on developments of economic and social issues in the United Nations. Points out potential changes in the international environment.
U.S. Council for International Business
1212 Avenue of the Americas
New York, NY 10036
(212) 354–4480

U.S. Customs and International Trade Guide
Peter Buck Feller

4 vols. Loose leaf. $200.00.
Subject heading: Customs administration—United States

Includes a current analysis of United States customs laws as well as texts on important customs regulations, tarrif schedules and customs forms.
Matthew Bender
DM Department
1275 Broadway
Albany, NY 12201
(518) 465–3575
(800) 833–3630

U.S. Export Weekly

Weekly. $315.00/year.
Subject heading: United States—Commerce—Periodicals
Library of Congress Call Number: HF1 .I66

The Bureau of National Affairs, Inc.
1231 25th Street, N.W.
Washington, DC 20037
(202) 452–4200

Wall Street Journal

5 times a week. $89.00/year.
Library of Congress Call Number: HG1 .W258

Wall Street Journal
Post Office Box 267
West Middlesex, PA 16159
(412) 528–1001

Washington International Business Report

Biweekly; loose leaf updates. $240.00/year.

Subject heading: Commerce—Periodicals

Provides an organization chart, the names and telephone numbers of key officials and the description of the responsibilities of the organization or committee of major government organizations and congressional committees. Includes the *Newsletter*, *Washington International Organizational Guide*, *Who's Who in International Washington*, and *Special Report*.

Washington International Business Report
Suite 717
1625 Eye Street, N.W.
Washington, DC 20006
(202) 872-8181

Washington International Business Report Service see **Washington International Business Report.**

Who's Who in International Organizations see **Yearbook of International Organizations.**

World Bank Atlas

1981. 16th ed. Annual. 24p. $2.50.

Subject heading: Gross national product—Maps

Three global maps provide the data on gross national product (GNP) per capita (1979); population (mid-1979); and GNP per capita and population growth rates (1970–1979) for countries and territories with populations of one million or more. Per capita GNP (1979) by major region is shown on a computer-generated map.

World Bank Headquarters
1818 H Street, N.W.
Washington, DC 20433
(202) 477–1234

World Bank Monthly Operational Summary see **Development Forum.**

World Business Perspectives

Bimonthly.

Subject heading: Commerce—Periodicals

Each issue of this newsletter discusses a world business situation, using

charts and graphs for illustration. Some recent topics covered include "Foreign Capital Expenditures by American Companies" and "World Commodity Markets."
Conference Board, Inc.
845 Third Avenue
New York, NY 10022
(212) 759–0900

World Development Report 1981
1981. 200p. $16.00.
Subject heading: Economic development—Periodicals
Library of Congress Call Number: HC59.7 .W659

The main theme of the report is the global and national adjustment necessary to promote sustainable growth in the changing world economy. Examines the effect of the inflation, recession, and rise in oil prices in the 1970s on developing countries. Economic growth in the 1970s and 1980s, trade and energy policies, external finance, country experience, and human development are also discussed.
World Bank
1818 H Street, N.W.
Washington, DC 20433
(202) 477–1234

World Energy Outlook see **The Organisation for Economic Cooperation and Development.**

World Statistics in Brief: United Nations Statistical Pocketbook
6th ed. Annual. $2.50.
Subject heading: Statistics

Contains basic statistics on the regions and nations of the world, including demographic, economic, agricultural, educational, and other key information on 156 countries.
UNIPUB
1180 Avenue of the Americas
New York, NY 10036
(212) 764–2791

World Trade and Business Digest
Monthly. $50.00.
Subject heading: International trade opportunities

Lists trade contacts, business news and investment opportunities worldwide.

Kassanga International of New York
213 East 88th Street
New York, NY 10028
(212) 427–7176

World Trade Annual

Annual.

Subject heading: Commerce—Yearbooks
Library of Congress Call Number: HF53 .W6

Walker and Company
720 Fifth Avenue
New York, NY 10019

World Trade Annual Supplement

Annual. $75.90/volume.

Subject heading: Commerce—Directories
Walker and Company
720 Fifth Avenue
New York, NY 10019

World Trade News

Monthly. $37.00/year.

Ivan R. Vernon, Director
World Trade Education Center
Cleveland State University
Cleveland, OH 44115
(216) 687–3733

Worldcasts

8 times a year. $1,200.00.

Predicasts
11001 Cedar Avenue
Cleveland, OH 44106
(800) 321–6388
(216) 795–3000
Notes: Regional editions (4 times a year), $800.00. Product editions (4 times a year), $800.00.

World-Wide Chamber of Commerce Directory

1982. Annual.

Subject heading: Boards of trade—Directories

Included in this book are lists such as Foreign Chambers of Commerce throughout the world; Foreign embassies and consulates in the United States; U.S. consulates and embassies overseas; key officers of foreign-service posts; and Foreign Consular offices in the United States.
Johnson Publishing Company, Inc.
Post Office Box 455
Eighth and Van Buren
Loveland, CO 80537
(303) 667–0652

Worldwide Economic Indicators
1982. Annual. $135.00.
Subject heading: Market surveys—Periodicals
Business International Corporation
One Dag Hammarskjold Plaza
New York, NY 10017
(212) 750–6300

Worldwide Marketing Horizons
Bimonthly. Free.
Subject heading: Export marketing—Periodicals
Pan American World Airways
Pan Am Building
New York, NY 10017
(212) 880–1234

Yearbook of Industrial Statistics
1977. 11th ed. 2 vols. $35.00.
Subject heading: Industry—Periodicals
Library of Congress Call Number: JX1977 .A2

United Nations Publications
Room A-3315
New York, NY 10017
(212) 244–1330

Yearbook of International Organizations 1981
1981. 19th ed. $125.00.
Subject heading: International officials and employers
Library of Congress Call Number: JX1995 .W49

Comprehensive reference work offering detailed descriptions of international organizations. Contains more than 8,000 current entries covering governmental and nongovernmental organizations, associations, com-

mittees, and so on which are international in their financial support, memberships, officers, and aims.
Gale Research Company
Book Tower
Detroit, MI 48226
(313) 961–2242

Yearbook of International Trade Statistics
Annual. 2 vols. $70.00.
Subject heading: Commercial statistics
Library of Congress Call Number: JX1977 .A2

Provides annual export-and-import statistics for over 150 countries, with analysis by commodity of imports and exports according to the Standard International Trade Classification. Comparative figures for several years are provided in tables. Volume 1 gives trade by country and contains an analysis of the flow of trade among countries and the price fluctuation of goods that move internationally. Volume 2 gives trade by commodity.
United Nations Publications
Room A-3315
New York, NY 10017
(212) 244–1330

Yearbook of Labor Statistics see **International Publications Services.**

Yearbook of National Accounts Statistics
Annual. $70.00.
Subject heading: National income—Periodicals
Library of Congress Call Number: HC79.I5 U53

This yearbook is published in three volumes with comparative economic data arranged by country contained in the first two. International tables are provided in the third volume. Figures for gross domestic products, exports and imports, industrial activity, wholesale and retail trade, and others are included.
United Nations Publications
Room A-3315
New York, NY 10017
(212) 244–1330

3 International Business Data Sources (Directories, Almanacs, Handbooks)

Balance of Payments Statistics
Monthly and yearbook. $33.00.
Subject heading: Balance of trade—Yearbooks

Provides statistics on goods and services, long-term and short-term capital, and reserves for over 110 countries.
International Monetary Fund
700 19th Street, N.W.
Washington, DC 20431
(202) 477–7000

Balance of Payments Yearbook see **Balance of Payments Statistics.**

Bankers Directory and Special List of Selected Lawyers see **Rand McNally International Bankers Directory.**

Book of World Rankings
George Thomas Kurian.
rev. ed. $24.95.
Subject heading: Statistics
Library of Congress Call Number: HA155 .K87 1983

Over 190 nations are compared and ranked on the basis of their performance in three hundred key areas. These areas include national income, exports, balance of trade, commodities produced, consumption per capita, and so on.
Facts on File, Inc.
119 West 57th Street
New York, NY 10019
(212) 683–2244

Bradford's Directory of Marketing Research Agencies and Management Consultants in the U.S. and the World
1978. 13th ed. $25.50.
Subject heading: Marketing research—Directories

Contains listing of over five hundred marketing-research firms.
Bradford's Directory of Marketing Research Agencies and Manufacturing

Consultants
Department B-15
Post Office Box 276
Fairfax, VA 22030
(703) 560–7484
Cross Reference and Notes: *Bradford's Survey and Directory of Marketing Research Agencies in the United States and the World.*

Bradford's Survey and Directory of Marketing Research Agencies in the United States and the World *see* **Bradford's Directory of Marketing Research Agencies and Management Consultants in the U.S. and the World.**

Brandnames: Who Owns What
Diane Waxer Frankenstein.
1981. 559p. $45.00.
Subject heading: United States—Manufacturers—Directories
Library of Congress Call Number: T12 .F72 1981

Reference book listing the manufacturers that produce more than 15,000 brand-name products. Provides company information such as location of headquarters, telephone number, chief executive, brief description of corporation, outstanding stock and exchange on which stock is traded. Contains listing of brand names produced by each company.
Facts on File, Inc.
Order Department
460 Park Avenue, South
New York, NY 10016
(212) 683–2244

Business Traveller's Handbook: A Guide to Europe
Edited by Jane Walker and Mark Ambrose.
$19.95 each.
Subject heading: Europe—Description and travel, 1945– —Guidebooks

This series of six books covers: (1) Asia, Australia, and the Pacific; (2) the Middle East; (3) Latin America; (4) Africa; (5) Europe; and (6) the United States and Canada. Each book includes information on import/export regulations, locations of major banks, entertainment and shopping hints, tipping customs, and so on.

Facts on File, Inc.
Order Department
460 Park Avenue, South
New York, NY 10016
(212) 683–2244

Canadian Key Business Directory
Library of Congress Call Number: HF3223 .C24

Canada's largest public and private businesses are listed.
Dun and Bradstreet of Canada
84 Carlton Street
Toronto, Ontario, Canada M5B 1L6

China Trade Handbook
Edited by Lawrence Fung.
1980. 312p. $49.95.
Subject heading: China—Commerce—Handbooks, manuals, etc.
Library of Congress Call Number: HF3837 .C45

Presents information on the Chinese economy, its industries, agriculture, services, finance, and trade.
Facts on File, Inc.
Order Department
460 Park Avenue, South
New York, NY 10016
(212) 683–2244

Corporate Handbook to the European Community
1981. $20.00.

Contains a practical introduction to the European Communities (EC) institutions and systems. Shows the relevance of understanding how the EC functions.
U.S. Council for International Business
1212 Avenue of the Americas
New York, NY 10036
(212) 354–4480

Countries of the World Current History Encyclopedia of Developing Nations
Edited by Carol L. Thompson, Mary M. Anderberg, and Joan B. Antell.
1982. 395p. $34.95.

Subject heading: Underdeveloped areas
Library of Congress Call Number: HC59.7 .C83

McGraw-Hill Book Company
1221 Avenue of the Americas
New York, NY 10020
(212) 997–1221

Diamond's Japan Business Directory 1981
1981. 15th ed. Annual. 469p. $335.00.
Subject heading: Japan—Industries—Directories
Library of Congress Call Number: HC461 .D5

Contains names of over 1,200 Japanese firms listed on the Tokyo Stock Exchange and gives a brief history of the company, officers and directors, financial statements, ten-year tables, and forecasts.
International Publications Service
114 East 32nd Street
New York, NY 10016
(212) 685–9351

A Dictionary of the European Economic Community
John Paxton.
1977. 287p. $20.00.
Subject heading: European Economic Community—Dictionaries
Library of Congress Call Number: HC241.2 .P378 1977b

Dictionary providing materials related to the EEC such as terms, treaties, and agreements.
Facts on File, Inc.
460 Park Avenue, South
New York, NY 10016
(212) 683–2244

Directory Information Service
3 times a year. $70.00/year.
Subject heading: Directories—Directories
Library of Congress Call Number: Z5771 .D55 Suppl.

Supplement to *Directory of Directories.*
Gale Research Company
Book Tower
Detroit, MI 48226
(313) 961–2242

Directory of American Business in Germany

1982. 9th ed. 661p. $55.00.
Subject heading: United States—Commerce—Germany (Federal Republic, 1949–)
Library of Congress Call Number: HF3099 .B3 1982

Contains listing of more than 4,500 German firms and their U.S. counterparts. Also provided are names of over 3,500 U.S. firms and their business partners in Germany. Includes a classified directory of supply sources.
International Publications Service
114 East 32nd Street
New York, NY 10016
(212) 685–9351

Directory of American Firms Operating in Foreign Countries

1979. 9th ed. $125.00.
Subject heading: Corporations, American—Directories
Library of Congress Call Number: HG4538.A1 D5

Section 1 lists over 4,500 American companies with the president's name, officer in charge of foreign operations, and countries of operation. Section 2 classifies companies according to country of operation.
World Trade Academy Press
50 East 42nd Street
New York, NY 10017
(212) 697–4999

The Directory of Business Information see **Directory of European Business Information Sources.**

Directory of Directories 1983

1982. 2nd ed. 990p. $90.00.
Subject heading: Directories—Directories
Library of Congress Call Number: Z5771 .D55

Approximately 7,000 directories described and indexed covering such topics as government, business, education, public affairs, foreign directories, and science.
Gale Research Company
Book Tower
Detroit, MI 48226
(313) 961–2242
Notes: Kept up to date by *Directory Information Service.*

The Directory of Europmarket Borrowers

301p. $45.00.

Subject heading: Foreign exchange brokers—Directories

Provides a listing of 1,000 borrowing institutions from over one hundred countries. Also contains the names of those responsible for international borrowing, their address, telex and telephone numbers, and their recent loans.

Marketing Manager
Euromoney Publications
Nestor House
Playhouse Yard
London EC4V 5EX England

Directory of European Associations

1979–1981. 2nd ed. 2 vols. $175.00/vol. 1; $130.00/vol. 2.

Subject heading: Trade and professional associations—Europe—Directories

Library of Congress Call Number: HD2429.E87 D57 1979

Part One contains information on more than 9,000 national and regional organizations of national significance. With the exception of Great Britain and Ireland, all countries of Europe are covered. Part Two covers approximately 6,000 associations and societies in areas such as natural sciences; technology; engineering and architecture; economic sciences, finance and business management; medicine, social sciences; and law.

Gale Research Company
Book Tower
Detroit, MI 48226
(313) 961–2242

Directory of European Business Information Sources

Edited by William A. Benjamin and Irene Kingston.

1980. 590p. $95.00.

Subject heading: Business—Information services—Europe—Directories

Ballinger Publishing Company
54 Church Street
Cambridge, MA 02138
(617) 492–0070

Directory of Foreign Firms Operating in the U.S.

Juvenal Londono Angel.

1978. 4th ed. 786p. $85.00.

Subject heading: Corporations, Foreign—United States—Directories
Library of Congress Call Number: HG4057 .A155 1978

World Trade Academy Press
50 East 42nd Street
New York, NY 10017
(212) 697–4999

Directory of Foreign Manufacturers in the United States
Jeffrey S. Arpan and David A. Ricks.
1979. 2nd ed. 303p. $34.95.
Subject heading: United States—Manufacturers—Directories
Library of Congress Call Number: HD9723 .A76 1979

Contains a listing of firms having U.S. and foreign addresses and products. An index of companies by state, a product index, and an index to parent companies by name and by country are also included.
Business Publishing Division
College of Business Administration
Georgia State University
University Plaza
Atlanta, GA 30303
(404) 658–4253

Directory of International Business Travel and Relocation see **International Business Travel and Relocation Directory.**

Directory of the Commission of the European Communities
1982. $2.75.
Subject heading: European cooperation—Directories
U.S. Information Office
Suite 707
2100 M Street, N.W.
Washington, DC 20037
(202) 862–9500

Encyclopedia of American Associations see **Encyclopedia of Associations: A Guide to National and International Organizations.**

Encyclopedia of Associations: A Guide to National and International Organizations
Edited by Denise Akew.

$150.00/vol. 1;
$135.00/vol. 2;
17th ed. 3 vols. $150.00/vol. 3.
Subject heading: Associations, institutions, etc.—Directories
Library of Congress Call Number: HS17 .G334 1982

Volume 1 lists national organizations of the United States and covers approximately 16,000 active organizations, arranged in seventeen subject categories. Volume 2 contains a geographic and executive index. Volume 3 lists new associations and projects.
Gale Research Company
Book Tower
Detroit, MI 48226
(313) 961–2242

Encyclopedia of Business Information Sources
Edited by Paul Wasserman, Charlotte Georgi, and James Way.
1980. 4th ed. 778p. $115.00.
Subject heading: Business—Information services
Library of Congress Call Number: HF5353 .E9 1980

A detailed listing of nearly 20,000 entries on 1,280 subjects and industries, including basic statistical sources, directories, almanacs, periodicals, associations, handbooks, bibliographies, dictionaries, general works, and so on.
Gale Research Company
Book Tower
Detroit, MI 48226
(313) 961–2242

Encyclopedia of Geographic Information Sources
Paul Wasserman.
1978. 3rd ed. 167p. $58.00.
Subject heading: Business—Information services
Library of Congress Call Number: HF5353 .E54 1978

This guide gives sources of information for states and cities and for certain foreign countries. Sources listed include directories, almanacs, periodicals, bibliographies, and so on. Formerly published as volume 2 of the *Encyclopedia of Business Information Sources.*
Gale Research Company
Book Tower
Detroit, MI 48226
(313) 961–2242

Encyclopedia of Information Systems and Services

Edited by Anthony T. Kruzas and John Schmittroth, Jr.
1981. 4th ed. 933p. $235.00.
Subject heading: Information services—United States—Directories
Library of Congress Call Number: Z674.3 .E52 1981

Contains in-depth descriptions of over 2,000 organizations producing, processing, storing, and using bibliographic and nonbibliographic information in the United States and sixty other countries. Also covers about 1,500 data bases of various types such as bibliographic, nonbibliographic, online, offline, commercial, governmental, and private.
Gale Research Company
Book Tower
Detroit, MI 48226
(313) 961–2242
Cross Reference and Notes: *New Information Systems and Services*. A periodical supplementing the basic volume describing new organizations, systems, and products as they are developed ($170.00).

Encyclopedia of the Third World

George Thomas Kurian.
Rev. ed. 3 vols. $125.00.
Subject heading: Underdeveloped areas—Dictionaries
Library of Congress Call Number: HC59.7 .K87 1982

Facts on File, Inc.
460 Park Avenue, South
New York, NY 10016
(212) 683–2244

Europe, An Exporter's Handbook

Compiled by Paul Jenner.
403p. $22.50.
Subject heading: Europe—Commerce—Handbooks, manuals, etc.
Library of Congress Call Number: HF3497 .E87 1981

Provides information on how to sell goods to the seventeen countries of Western Europe.
Facts on File, Inc.
Order Department
460 Park Avenue, South
New York, NY 10016
(212) 683–2244

European Historical Statistics, 1750–1975

1980. 868p. $85.00.

Subject heading: Europe—Statistics—History

Library of Congress Call Number: HA1107 .M5 1980

Furnishes pertinent historical statistics of various countries taken from official publications including population and vital statistics, labor force, agriculture, industry, external trade, transport and communications, finance, prices, education, and national accounts.

Facts on File, Inc.
460 Park Avenue, South
New York, NY 10016
(212) 683–2244

European Marketing Data and Statistics 1982

18th ed. $180.00.

Subject heading: Europe—Statistics

Library of Congress Call Number: HA1107 .E87

Annual volume providing up-to-date, statistical data on twenty-six European countries. Areas covered in the volume's fifteen major sections include: population, employment, production, trade, economy, standard of living, consumer expenditures, and consumption.

Gale Research Company
Book Tower
Detroit, MI 48226
(313) 961–2242

Europe's Largest Companies

1982.

Includes 7,500 industrial companies and 2,000 trading companies, transport companies, banks, insurance companies, hotels, restaurant chains, and advertising agencies.

Dun and Bradstreet International
Three Century Drive
Parsippany, NJ 07054
(800) 526–0651
(201) 455–0061

Exporters' Encyclopedia: World Marketing Guide

1982. Annual. Kept up to date by supplementary bulletins issued twice monthly. $325.00.

Subject heading: United States—Commerce

Provides pertinent data for doing business in certain countries, including import-and-exchange regulations, shipping information, and so on.
Dun and Bradstreet
Post Office Box 3224
Church Street Station
New York, NY 10008

External Trade Statistics: User's Guide
1982. $4.00.
European Community Information Center
Suite 707
2100 M Street, N.W.
Washington, DC 20037
(202) 862–9500

The Financing of Exports and Imports: A Guide to Procedures
1980. 48p. Free.
Subject heading: Letters of credit
Library of Congress Call Number: HG3745 .M67 1980

Morgan Guaranty Trust Company of New York
International Banking Division
23 Wall Street
New York, NY 10015
(212) 483–2323

Foreign Commerce Handbook
1981. 17th ed. 274p. $10.00.
Subject heading: Commerce—Handbooks, manuals, etc.

Information on all phases of international business is covered in this reference source, including foreign-trade services, daily language of foreign commerce, bibliography, and lists of organizations.
International Division
Chamber of Commerce of the United States
1615 H Street, N.W.
Washington, DC 20062
(202) 659–6000

Foreign Trade Marketplace
Edited by George J. Schultz.
1977. 1st ed. 662p. $78.00.

Subject heading: Commerce—Handbooks, manuals, etc.
Library of Congress Call Number: HF1010 .F67

Provides a broad, comprehensive view of the mechanics of trade for U.S. companies. Descriptive chapters on buying and selling in foreign markets are combined with directories of companies and organizations essential to trade.
Gale Research Company
Book Tower
Detroit, MI 48226
(313) 961–2242

The Global Guide to the World of Business
David Hoopes.
1981. 608p. $45.00.
Subject heading: Commerce—Information services—Directories
Library of Congress Call Number: HF54.5 .H66

Reference source containing the names and addresses of every appropriate private organization, government bureau and information agency dealing with international business. Also provided are descriptions of the types of information and sources provided by each organization and the names and addresses necessary for locating publications, documents, films, and special services.
Facts on File, Inc.
Order Department
460 Park Avenue, South
New York, NY 10016
(212) 683–2244

Glossary: International Economic Organizations and Terms
Forthcoming. $10.00.

Reference source on international operations containing listings of intergovernmental bodies, international associations, and acronyms and terms frequently used in international operations.
U.S. Council for International Business
1212 Avenue of the Americas
New York, NY 10036
(212) 354–4490

Green Book—International Directory of Marketing Research Houses and Services
$30.00.
Subject heading: Marketing research—Directories

Contains a listing of 935 marketing research firms in fifty countries, plus a brief description of each company.
American Marketing Association
420 Lexington Avenue
New York, NY 10017
(212) 687-3280

Guide to Key British Enterprises see **Key British Enterprises: The Top 20,000 British Companies.**

Handbook of International Business
Edited by Ingo Walter and Tracy Murray.
1982. 1,312p. $55.00.
Subject heading: International business enterprises—Management—Handbooks, manuals, etc.
Library of Congress Call Number: HD62.4 .H36 1982

Covers international business environment, trade, finance, legal issues, business and marketing, and operations management.
John Wiley and Sons
605 Third Avenue
New York, NY 10158
(212) 850-6418

Handbook of International Trade and Development Statistics
1979. $44.00.
Subject heading: Underdeveloped areas—Commerce
Library of Congress Call Number: JX1977 .A2 1979

Provides statistical data pertinent to the examination of the problems of world trade and development. Topics covered include commodity prices, imports and exports, value of world trade by regions and countries, balance of payments, indicators of development, and a ranking of countries according to per capita GNP.
United Nations
Sales Section
Publishing Division
New York, NY 10017
(212) 244-1330

International Bankers Directory see **Rand McNally International Bankers Directory.**

International Business Travel and Relocation Directory

1982. 2nd ed. 896p. $185.00.

Subject heading: Americans in foreign countries—Employment—Handbooks, manuals, etc.

Library of Congress Call Number: HF5549.5.E45 I57 1981

Two-part guidebook for international business travel and operations. Part One provides information concerning personnel guidelines for choosing the right person for extended overseas assignments, and information they will need on moving to a foreign country designed specifically for employees moving abroad. Part Two provides resource and reference materials for Africa, Asia, Europe, Middle East/North Africa, and the Western Hemisphere.

Gale Research Company
Book Tower
Detroit, MI 48226
(313) 961–2242

The International Dictionary of Business

Hano Johannsen and G. Terry Page.

1981. 376p. $17.95.

Subject heading: Management—Dictionaries

Library of Congress Call Number: HD30.15 .J64 1981

Prentice-Hall, Inc.
Box 500
Englewood Cliffs, NJ 07632
(201) 592–2000

The International Directory of Corporate Affiliations

1982. 802p. $127.00.

Subject heading: Corporations—Directories

A comprehensive reference source to foreign companies with U.S. holdings and U.S. companies with foreign holdings.

National Register Publishing Company
5201 Old Orchard Road
Skokie, IL 60077
(312) 470–3100

International Directory of Management see **International Directory of Business.**

International Foundation Directory

1979. 2nd ed. 378p. $65.00.

Subject heading: Endowments—Directories
Library of Congress Call Number: HV7 .I57 1979

Completely revised and updated edition of IFD concentrating on foundations, trusts, and other related nonprofit institutions that operate internationally. Covers 686 institutions, including selected national foundations located throughout the world. Gives full name and address, founding date, history, description of activities, financial data, names of officers, and publications for most entries.
Gale Research Company
Book Tower
Detroit, MI 48226
(313) 961–2242

International Hotel Guide 1982
1982. 35th ed. 523p. $30.00.
Subject heading: Hotels, taverns, etc.—Directories

Provides listing of IHA member hotels and restaurants throughout the world giving descriptions of facilities and rates.
International Publications Service
114 East 32nd Street
New York, NY 10016
(212) 685–9351

International Marketing Data and Statistics 1981
1982. 7th ed. $180.00.
Subject heading: Statistics—Periodicals
Library of Congress Call Number: HA42 .I56 1982

Comparative statistical data on a hundred countries located in Asia, Africa, Australia, and the Americas are provided in this companion to *European Marketing Data and Statistics 1981.* Includes information on population, employment, production, trade, economy, standard of living, consumption, communication, and more.
Gale Research Company
Book Tower
Detroit, MI 48226
(313) 961–2242

International Marketing Handbook 1981
Edited by Frank E. Bair.
1981. 1st ed. 2 vols.; 2,380p. $140.00/set.
Subject heading: Export marketing—Handbooks, manuals, etc.
Library of Congress Call Number: HF1009.5 .I537

Provides current government reports of marketing profiles for 138 nations. Reports provide information such as foreign-trade outlook, industry trends, transportation and utilities, distribution and sales channels, and advertising. Supplementary material includes trade guides to the European Common Market, the Near East, and North Africa.
Gale Research Company
Book Tower
Detroit, MI 48226
(313) 961–2242

The International Relations Directory
Jack C. Plano and Roy Olton.
1982. $19.75.
Subject heading: International relations—Dictionaries
Library of Congress Call Number: JX1226 .P55 1982

ABC-CLIO
Riviera Campus
2040 A.P.S.
Post Office Box 4397
Santa Barbara, CA 93103
(805) 963–4221

International Research Centers Directory
1st ed. $145.00.
Subject heading: Research institutes—Directories
Library of Congress Call Number: Q179.98 .I58

Gale Research Company
Book Tower
Detroit, MI 48226
(313) 961–2242

The International Who's Who 1982–1983
1982. 46th ed. 1,426p. $120.00.

Contains biographical information on outstanding men and women throughout the world. Information on people well known in international affairs, government, diplomacy, science, business, law, and so on.
UNIPUB
1180 Avenue of the Americas
New York, NY 10036
(212) 764–2791

Jaeger's Europa-Register-Teleurope 1982
1981. 26th ed. 977p. $65.00.
Subject heading: Europe—Industries—Directories
Library of Congress Call Number: HC240 .J34

Over 190,000 manufacturers, importers, exporters, and service industries in thirty European countries are listed in this annual.
International Publications Service
114 East 32nd Street
New York, NY 10016
(212) 685–9351

Key British Enterprises: The Top 20,000 British Companies
1981.
Subject heading: Great Britain—Industries—Directories
Dun and Bradstreet Ltd.
6–8 Bonhill Street
London EC2A 4BU England

Key Words in International Trade
1981. 152p. $20.00.
Subject heading: Business—Terminology

Translates over 1,000 technical terms dealing with international trade into four foreign languages (German, Spanish, French, and Italian). Includes index in each of these languages.
The ICC Publishing Corporation, Inc.
Suite 300
125 East 23rd Street
New York, NY 10010

Latin America Market Guide
Semiannual.

Essential business facts on companies in Middle and South America are provided.
Dun and Bradstreet International
Sales Division
U.S. Operations Office
Suite 9069
One World Trade Center
New York, NY 10048
(212) 938–8400

Lloyd's Maritime Directory 1982

1982. 1st ed. Annual. 1,200p. $95.00.
Subject heading: Ship building—Directories

Up-to-date, in-depth information on more than 34,000 vessels and over 5,000 shipowners and managers with their addresses, telephone and telex numbers. In addition, ship builders, ship repairers, towage and salvage companies, and worldwide maritime organizations are listed.
International Publications Service
114 East 32nd Street
New York, NY 10016
(212) 685–9351

The Multilingual Commercial Directory

1978. 332p. $22.50.
Subject heading: Computers—Dictionaries—Polyglot
Library of Congress Call Number: QA76.15 .I78

Contains a selection of 3,000 of the most frequently used terms in international business in six languages.
Facts on File, Inc.
460 Park Avenue, South
New York, NY 10016
(212) 683–2244

Multinational Corporations: The ECSIM Guide for Information Sources

Edited by Joseph O. Mekeirle.
1978. 454p. $79.50.
Subject heading: International business enterprises—Bibliography
Library of Congress Call Number: Z7164.T87 E95 1977

Sourcebook providing a current listing of all phases of information on multinational corporations and related issues. Points out where books, reports, articles, data, statistics, and facts and figures concerning multinationals can be found.
Praeger Publishers
Division of Holt Rinehart and Winston/CBS
521 Fifth Avenue
New York, NY 10175
(212) 599–8413

New Information Systems and Services see **Encyclopedia of Information Systems and Services.**

Owen's Commerce and Travel and International Register see **Owen's Trade Directory: Business Travel Guide.**

Owen's Trade Directory: Business Travel Guide
1982. 29th ed. Annual. 1,250p. $75.00.
Library of Congress Call Number: HF3872 .P3

Provides basic economic information for sixty-five countries in the Middle East and Arabian Gulf, Southeast Asia and the Far East, Africa, the Mediterranean, and the West Indies. Also contains a listing of manufacturers, importers, hotels, airlines, and banks in each country.
International Publications Service
114 East 32nd Street
New York, NY 10016
(212) 685–9351

Rand McNally International Bankers Directory
Semiannual. $135.00.
Subject heading: Bankers—United States—Directories
Library of Congress Call Number: HG2441 .R3

Contains a geographical listing of U.S. and principal foreign banks. Also provides a listing of officers, directors, and balance-sheet data for each.
Rand McNally and Company
Financial Publishing Division
Post Office Box 7600
Chicago, IL 60680
(312) 673–9100

Reference Book for World Traders
Ulrich Horst and Edward Croner.
1981. 2 vols. Loose leaf. $91.95/year including postage.
Subject heading: Commerce—Handbooks, manuals, etc.
Library of Congress Call Number: HF1010 .C66

Provides information necessary for planning exporting and importing and market research.
Croner Publications, Inc.
211-03 Jamaica Avenue
Queens Village
New York, NY 11428
(212) 464–0866
Note: Kept up to date by an amendment service.

Salaries Worldwide 1982

$3,750.00. Entire study.

Survey of executive compensation that is available for twenty-five countries. Price varies according to number purchased.
Business International
World Headquarters
One Dag Hammarskjold Plaza
New York, NY 10017
(212) 750–6300

Statesman Year-Book

John Paxton.
1981. 118th ed. 1,696p. $30.00.
Subject heading: Political science—Yearbooks

Provides data on constitution and government, population, finance, defense, industries and commerce, transportation, banking, and so on for every country.
Saint Martin's Press, Inc.
175 Fifth Avenue
New York, NY 10010
(212) 674–5151

Statistical Abstract of Latin America

1981. Annual. $47.50.
Subject heading: Latin America—Statistics

Contains statistics for each Latin American country on population, vital statistics, social indicators, economics, and finance.
University of California
Latin America Center
405 Hilgard Avenue
Los Angeles, CA 90024
(213) 825–6634

Statistical Yearbook

$50.00.

Subject heading: Statistics—Periodicals
Library of Congress Call Number: HA12.5 .U63

Statistical data for member countries of the United Nations Educational, Scientific and Cultural Organization. Includes tables for education, science and technology, culture and communication, and so on.

United Nations Publications
Room A-3315
New York, NY 10017
(212) 244–1330

Statistics Europe: Guide for the Market Researcher to 34 Countries in Europe
Joan M. Harvey.
1976. 3rd ed. $55.00.

The chief sources of statistical information for each European country are described.
International Publications Service
114 East 32nd Street
New York, NY 10016
(212) 685–9351

Statistics Sources
Edited by Paul Wasserman, Jacqueline O'Brien, Daphne A. Grace, and Kenneth Clansky.
1982. 7th ed. 1,388p. $130.00.
Subject heading: Statistics—Bibliography
Library of Congress Call Number: Z7551 .S84 1982

Subject guide to information on industrial, business, social, educational, financial, and other subjects for the United States and worldwide. Entries are included under both country's name and subject.
Gale Research Company
Book Tower
Detroit, MI 48226
(313) 961–2242

Stores of the World Directory 1982/83
1982. 13th ed. 1,180p. $135.00.
Subject heading: Commerce—Directories
Library of Congress Call Number: HF54.G7 S8

More than 7,000 department stores, supermarkets, and chains in 121 countries are listed alphabetically by country, with addresses, telephone numbers, and names of chief executives and buyers.
International Publications Service
114 East 32nd Street
New York, NY 10016
(212) 685–9351

Who Owns Whom

2 vols.

Subject heading: Corporations—Europe—Directories
Library of Congress Call Number: HG4132.Z5 W5

A four-part series: United Kingdom and Republic of Ireland, continental Europe, Australia and Far East, and North America. Contains current data showing the ownership of subsidiary and associate companies and how they fit into the parent group.
Dun's Marketing Services
Dun and Bradstreet Corporation
Three Century Drive
Parsippany, NJ 07054
(800) 526–0651
(201) 455–0061

Who Owns Whom: Continental Edition see **Who Owns Whom.**

World Currency Charts

Free.

Subject heading: Money—Tables
Library of Congress Call Number: HG3863 .A65

Contains charts and statistics that provide exchange rates per U.S. dollars for the currencies in 147 countries. Data is provided from 1929 to the most recent year available when the book is published.
American International Investment Corporation
3258 Paloma Court
Coulterville, CA 95311

World Directory of Fertilizer Manufacturers
1981. 5th ed. $220.00.
Subject heading: Fertilizer industry—Directories
Library of Congress Call Number: HD9483.A2 B7 1981

Contains a geographical listing of fertilizer manufacturers worldwide. Also provides a directory of purchasing organizations and a list of major international trading and sales organizations.
International Publications Service
114 East 32nd Street
New York, NY 10016
(212) 685–9351

The World Directory of Multinational Enterprises
John M. Stopford, John H. Dunning, and Klaus O. Haberich.
2 vols. $195.00

Subject heading: International business enterprises—Directories
Library of Congress Call Number: HD2755.5 .S843

Two-volume reference source that lists the six hundred largest multinationals in the world.
Facts on File, Inc.
Order Department
460 Park Avenue, South
New York, NY 10016
(212) 683–2244

World Guide to Abbreviations of Organizations
Edited by F.A. Buttress.
1981. 6th ed. 464p. $100.00.
Subject heading: Associations, institutions, etc.—Abbreviations
Library of Congress Call Number: A58 .B8 1981

A reference book that provides the complete names of companies, institutions, international agencies, and governmental departments throughout the world that are usually identified by initials or abbreviations. Contains approximately 27,500 entries.
Gale Research Company
Book Tower
Detroit, MI 48226
(313) 961–2242

World Guide to Trade Associations
1980. 2nd ed. 845p. $180.00.
Subject heading: Trade and professional associations—Directories
Library of Congress Call Number: HD2421 .W67

Gale Research Company
Book Tower
Detroit, MI 48226
(313) 961–2242

The World in Figures
1981. 294p. $27.50.
Subject heading: Statistics
Library of Congress Call Number: HA161 .W67 1980

Detailed statistics for every country in the world are provided, including information on location, rates of exchange, growth rates, resources, production, trade, and so on.

Facts on File, Inc.
119 West 57th Street
New York, NY 10019
(212) 683–2244

World Index of Economic Forecasts
G.R. Cyriax.
2nd ed. 378p. $95.00.
Subject heading: Economic forecasting—Directories
Library of Congress Call Number: HB3730 .W66 1981

The activities, techniques, and published output of the world's outstanding economic forecasters and forecasting institutions are covered. Contains 175 entries, with each participant providing details of forecasts of their domestic economies and their international average.
Facts on File, Inc.
Order Department
460 Park Avenue, South
New York, NY 10016
(212) 683–2244

World Tables 1980
2nd ed. 474p. $20.00.
Subject heading: Economic history, 1971–
Library of Congress Call Number: HC59 .I4989 1980

Reference source designed to make the comparative economic data used by the bank accessible to the business world. Tables cover the period between 1950 and 1973. Includes statistics on foreign trade, government indicators, demographic characteristics, and current revenue.
Johns Hopkins University Press
Order Department—Business Office
Baltimore, MD 21218
(301) 338–7861

World Trade Directory/Ohio
Forthcoming.
World Trade Education Center
Cleveland State University
Cleveland, OH 44115
(216) 687–3733

4 International Business Books (Marketing, Finance, Economics)

Adjustment and Financing in the Developing World: The Role of the International Monetary Fund
Edited by Tony Killick.
1982. $12.00.
Subject heading: Underdeveloped areas—Balance of payments—Congresses
Library of Congress Call Number: HG3890 .A38 1982

Results of a seminar on the problems facing the developing world in the present global environment of high inflation rates and large payment imbalances.
International Monetary Fund
Publications Unit, Room C-200
700 19th Street, N.W.
Washington, DC 20431
(202) 477–2945

American Foreign Policy
Valentine J. Belfiglio.
1982. 2nd ed. 142p. $9.00.
Subject heading: United States—Foreign relations
Library of Congress Call Number: JX1407 .B38 1982

College-level introductory text for courses in American foreign policy. Examines strategies and policies developed by American government leaders in relation to international organizations and other countries in light of the impact of subnational and national concerns, contemporary history, and American institutions.
University Press of America
Post Office Box 19101
Washington, DC 20036
(301) 459–3366

Analysis of Trade Between the European Community and the ACP States
1979. 531p. $30.00.
Subject heading: Commercial statistics

European Community Information Services
Suite 707
2100 M Street, N.W.
Washington, DC 20037
(202) 862–9500

Analysis of Trade Between the European Community and the Arab League Countries
1981. 534p. $40.40.
Subject heading: Arab countries—Commerce—European Economic Community countries—Statistics
European Community Information Service
Suite 707
2100 M Street, N.W.
Washington, DC 20037
(202) 862–9500

Analysis of Trade Between the European Community and the Latin American Countries 1965–1980
1981. $12.70.
European Community Information Service
Suite 707
2100 M Street, N.W.
Washington, DC 20037
(202) 862–9500

Another Look at Multinationals
1980.
The Conference Board
845 Third Avenue
New York, NY 10022
(212) 759–0900

The Art of Japanese Management: Applications for American Executives
Richard Tanner Pascale and Anthony G. Athos.
221p.
Subject heading: Management—United Staes
Library of Congress Call Number: HD70.U5 P3

Warner Books, Inc.
75 Rockefeller Plaza
New York, NY 10019
(212) 484–8000

Arthur Anderson and Company

Arthur Anderson and Company publishes many booklets useful to the international businessman. Some of these are:

Pocket Guide to European Corporate Taxes

The U.S./U.K. Double Tax Treaty

Asia and the Pacific . . . A Tax Tour

Arthur Anderson and Company
Distribution Clerk
69 West Washington Street
Chicago, IL 60602

Assessing Country Risk

1981. 172p. $85.00.
Subject heading: Developing countries—Finance

Textbook that focuses on assessing the risks involved in operating in a foreign country. Provides explanations of how to incorporate those assessments in planning, management, and investment decisions.
Beverly Dewar, Marketing Manager
Euromoney Publications
Nestor House
Playhouse Yard
London EC4V 5EX England

Assessing the Political Environment: An Emerging Function in International Companies

1980. 72p. $45.00.
Subject heading: Investments, foreign—Political aspects
Library of Congress Call Number: HG4538 .B53

The Conference Board
845 Third Avenue
New York, NY 10022
(212) 759–0900

Bank of America International Services

1981.

Provides an overview of the various services offered by the Bank of America. Also includes addresses of U.S. Department of Commerce field offices, Foreign Chamber of Commerce and Associations in the United States, American Chambers of Commerce abroad, and the branches of the

Bank of America. In addition, the booklet contains information on Incoterms, Uniform Customs and Practice for Documentary Credits, Letters of Credit, and so on.
Bank of America
International Banking Office
37-41 Broad Street
Post Office Box 466
Church Street Station
New York, NY 10015

The Basic Business Library: Core Resources
Bernard Schlessinger.
1983.
Subject heading: Business libraries
Library of Congress Call Number: Z675.B8 B37 1983

Section one contains full bibliographic data and prices for basic business references that libraries should have. Section two contains an annotated bibliography (last five years) of materials on business reference. The final section provides a series of papers on various business reference topics written by experts. Topics include selection, acquisitions, the reference process, government publications, financial services, and business information data bases.
Orynx Press
2214 North Central Avenue
Phoenix, AZ 85004
(602) 254–6156

A Bibliography of Business and Economic Forecasting
Edited by Robert Fildes, David Dews, and Syd Howell.
424p. $35.00.
Subject heading: Business forecasting—Indexes
Library of Congress Call Number: Z7164.C81 F39

Bibliography providing a comprehensive list of reference material appropriate to the selection of the best forecasting model for a particular situation; 3,200 references from thirty journals are included.
Facts on File, Inc.
Order Department
460 Park Avenue, South
New York, NY 10016
(212) 683–2244

Borrowing in International Markets
1977.
The Conference Board
845 Third Avenue
New York, NY 10022
(212) 759–0900

Business and the Middle East: Threats and Prospects
Edited by Robert A. Kilmarx and Yonah Alexander.
1982. 240p. $24.50.
Subject heading: Near East—Economic conditions—Address, essays, lectures.
Library of Congress Call Number: HC415.15 .B87 1982

Describes the various political, economic, and social situations that affect business in the Middle East.
Pergamon Press
Maxwell House
Fairview Park
Elmsford, NY 10523
(914) 592–7700

Business Information Sources
Lorna M. Daniells.
1976. $19.95.
Subject heading: Business—Bibliography
Library of Congress Call Number: Z7164.C81 D16

University of California Press
2223 Fulton Street
Berkeley, CA 94720
(415) 642–4247

Business Organizations and Agencies Directory
Edited by Anthony T. Kruzas and Robert C. Thomas.
1980. 1st ed. 890p. $130.00.
Subject heading: United States—Commerce—Directories
Library of Congress Call Number: HF3010 .B87

Covers various business organizations, agencies, associations, trade centers, and offices that provide current information in their particular fields. A wide range of modern business activity is covered, with listings of both U.S. and foreign organizations.

Gale Research Company
Book Tower
Detroit, MI 48226
(313) 961–2242

A Businessman's Guide to the GATT Customs Valuation Code
Saul L. Sherman and Hinrich Glashoff.
$33.00.
Subject heading: Tariff—Law and legislation

Comprehensive handbook published by the International Chamber of Commerce explaining changes in customs valuation. Kept up to date by annual supplements that summarize the latest changes in the field.
The ICC Publishing Corporation, Inc.
1212 Avenue of the Americas
New York, NY 10036
(212) 354–4480

Carnet: Move Goods Duty-Free Through Customs
United States Council for International Business
1212 Avenue of the Americas
New York, NY 10036

The Changing Character of Financial Management in Europe
1979.
The Conference Board
845 Third Avenue
New York, NY 10022
(202) 759–0900

Cities in the Developing World: Policies for Their Equitable and Efficient Growth
Johannes F. Linn.
1982. 352p. $27.50.

Describes the significant policy issues that occur during efforts to adapt to the growth of cities in developing countries. Also contains discussions of policies designed to increase the efficiency and equity of urban development. Specific areas covered are urban employment, income redistribution, transport, housing, and social services.
Oxford University Press, Inc.
200 Madison Avenue
New York, NY 10016
(212) 679–7300

Commodity Exports and Economic Development: The Commodity Problem and Policies in Developing Countries
F. Gerard Adams and Jere R. Behrman.
1982. 328p.
Subject heading: Commodity control
Library of Congress Call Number: HF1428 .A3 1982

Provides a description of a macroeconometric model used for evaluating the complex impact of fluctuations in commodity prices on producing countries' economies. Models of aggregate country, producing sectors and primary-commodity markets are presented.
Lexington Books
125 Spring Street
Lexington, MA 02173
(800) 428–8071

Comparison Advertising: A Worldwide Study
J.J. Boddewyn and Katherin Marton.
1978. $12.50.
Subject heading: Advertising, comparison
Library of Congress Call Number: HF5287 .B577

Hastings House Publications, Inc.
10 East 40th Street
New York, NY 10016
(212) 689–5400

Countries of the World and Their Leaders Yearbook 1982
5th ed. 2 vols., 1,265p. $58.00/set.
Subject heading: Geography
Library of Congress Call Number: G122 .C67 1979

This book contains the State Department's *Background Notes on Countries of the World*, which provide essential data on 168 nations and territories. Also featured are the State Department's *Status of the World's Nations*, a directory of foreign officials, and special reports on the operations, aims, and organization of the United Nations, CENTO, NATO, OAU, OECD, and the European Communities.
Gale Research Company
Book Tower
Detroit, MI 48226
(313) 961–2242

Note: Updated by semiannual supplement ($32.00).

Currency Risk

$85.00.

Covers the measurement and management of currency risk and analyzes various methods for defining and measuring exposure. Topics discussed include: hedging policies, objectives, and strategies and the techniques available to the treasurer, the Eurocurrency markets, a foreign-exchange reserve, and currency swaps.
Marketing Manager
Euromoney Publications
Nestor House
Playhouse Yard
London EC4U 5EX England

Currency Translation and Performance Evaluation in Multinationals
Helen Gernon Morsicato.
1980. 177p. $29.95.
Subject heading: International business enterprises—Accounting
Library of Congress Call Number: HF5686.I56 M67 1980

UMI Research Press
Ann Arbor, MI 48109

Development Strategies in Semi-Industrial Economies
Bela Balassa.
1982. 394p. $32.50.
Subject heading: Economic development—Case studies
Library of Congress Call Number: HD82 .B234 1982

Development strategies in semi-industrial economies that have established an industrial base are analyzed. Attempts to quantify the systems of incentives that are implemented in six semi-industrial developing economies—Argentina, Colombia, Israel, Korea, Singapore, and Taiwan. Also indicates the effects of the incentive systems on economic growth, international trade, and the allocation of resources.
The Johns Hopkins University Press
Baltimore, MD 21218

EC-China: A Statistical Analysis of Foreign Trade 1970–1979
1981. $10.50.
European Community Information Center
Suite 707
2100 M Street, N.W.
Washington, DC 20037
(202) 862–9500

EC-World Trade: A Statistical Analysis 1963–1979

1981. $22.40.

European Community Information Center
Suite 707
2100 M Street, N.W.
Washington, DC 20037
(202) 862–9500

EIU World Commodity Outlooks

$84.00 each including airmail.

One volume covers industrial raw materials (1983). Another volume covers food, feedstuffs, and beverages (1983).

The Economist Intelligence Unit
75 Rockefeller Plaza
New York, NY 10019
(212) 541–5730

EIU World Outlook 1983

$84.00 including airmail.

Subject heading: Economic history, 1945– —Periodicals
Library of Congress Call Number: HC59.E387 1983

Provides in-depth forecasts of probable trends in the economies of over 160 countries.

The Economist Intelligence Unit
75 Rockefeller Plaza
New York, NY 10019
(212) 541–5730

East Asia: Dimensions of International Business

Phillip D. Grub, Tan Chwee Huat, Kwan Kuen-Chor, and George H. Rott.

$7.60.

Focuses on introducing the businessman to the changing nature and global outreach of Asian business and finance. Contains articles on the changing pace of financial structures in Asia, export-marketing strategies, transnational data flows, Japanese productivity, and an economic outlook for China.

Credo (Malaysia) Sdn. Bhd.
1011, President House
Jalan Sultan Ismail
Kula Lampur, West Malaysia

Economic Environment of International Business
Raymond Vernon and Louis T. Wells, Jr.
1981. 3rd ed. 246p. $14.95.
Subject heading: International business enterprises—Management
Library of Congress Call Number: HD62.4 .V47 1981

Prentice-Hall, Inc.
Box 500
Englewood Cliffs, NJ 67632
(201) 592–2000

Economics and Foreign Policy: A Guide to Information Sources
Mark R. Amstutz.
1977. 179p. $36.00.
Subject heading: International economic relations—Bibliography
Library of Congress Call Number: Z7164.E17 A48

Gale Research Company
Book Tower
Detroit, MI 48226
(313) 961–2242

Electricity Pricing: Theory and Case Studies
Mohan Munasinghe and Jeremy J. Warford.
1982. 381p. $22.50.
Subject heading: Electric utilities—Asia, Southeastern—Rates

Provides a description of the underlying theory and practical application of power-pricing policies that maximize the net economic benefits of electricity consumption to society. A framework for analyzing system costs and setting tariffs is provided in the methodology, which permits the tariff to be revised on a continual basis. The application of the methodology to real systems is described in case studies of electricity-pricing exercises in Indonesia, Pakistan, the Philippines, Sri Lanka, and Thailand.
The Johns Hopkins University Press
Baltimore, MD 21218
(301) 338–7861

Employment and Manower Information in Developing Countries
1982. 150p. $8.55.

Training guide consisting of eighteen learning elements on the uses of EMI and the planning of national EMI programs and their implementation.

International Labor Office
Suite 330A
1750 New York Avenue, N.W.
Washington, DC 20006
(202) 376–2315

Employment Policy in Developing Countries: A Survey of Issues and Evidence
Lyn Squire.
1981. 229p. $16.95.
Subject heading: Underdeveloped areas—Labor supply
Library of Congress Call Number: HD5852 .S65

The three main issues addressed in this study are the low rates of growth in industrial employment, high rates of unemployment among new entrants to the urban labor market, and low levels of labor productivity and remuneration. The author points out inappropriate policies that have constrained the growth of labor demand and advanced labor supply. Industrial trade policy, agricultural growth, and the operation of capital markets are discussed on the demand side. Attention is focused on population and education policy on the supply side.
Oxford University Press, Inc.
200 Madison Avenue
New York, NY 10016
(212) 679–7300

Environmental Cooperation Among Industrialized Countries: The Role of Regional Organizations
Nancy K. Hetzel.
381p. $13.50.
Subject heading: Environmental policy—International Cooperation
Library of Congress Call Number: HC79.E5 H48

Contains an analysis of the evolution of intergovernmental cooperation on environmental issues among industrialized countries during the last ten years in five regional and subregional organizations: ECE, OECD, European communities, Council of Europe, and the Council for Mutual Assistance.
University Press of America
Post Office Box 19101
Washington, DC 20036
(301) 459–3366

Ernst and Whinney International Series

Free.

Brief booklets on approximately twenty-five countries. Booklets contain summarizations of various factors affecting trade and investment in the countries.
Ernst and Whinney International Operations
153 East 53rd Street
New York, NY 10022
(212) 888–9100
Note: Updated every one to two years.

The Eurodollar Bond Market
F.G. Fisher III.
200p. $65.00.
Subject heading: Euro-bond market
Library of Congress Call Number: HG3896 .F57

Provides an in-depth analysis of: the principal borrowers, investors and institutions in the market; issuing terms; new instruments; price and yield behavior; bringing a new issue to market; hybrid financing instruments; important related markets; and so on.
Beverley Dewar, Marketing Manager
Euromoney Publications
Nestor House
Playhouse Yard
London EC4V 5EX England

European Industrial Policy: Past, Present and Future
Lawrence G. Franko.
1980. 64p.
Subject heading: Industry and state—European Economic Community countries
The Conference Board
845 Third Avenue
New York, NY 10022
(212) 759–0900

The European Multinationals
Lawrence G. Franko.
1976. 276p. $16.95.
Subject heading: Corporations, foreign—Europe
Library of Congress Call Number: HD2844 .F7 1976

Greylock Publishers
13 Spring Street
Stamford, CT 06901

Europe's Population: Major Trends and Implications
1979.
The Conference Board
845 Third Avenue
New York, NY 10022
(212) 759–0900

The Expatriate Investor see **International Investing.**

Export Development Strategies
Michael R. Czinkota.
1982. 151p. $19.95.
Subject heading: Foreign trade promotion—United States
Library of Congress Call Number: HF1455 .C95 1982

Policies and programs necessary to improve U.S. export performance are discussed and the specific needs of groups of exporting firms are investigated. Creative export assistance programs are developed that are responsive to the differing needs of the groups. Guidelines are provided for the primary change agents, the U.S. Department of Commerce and the firm itself.
Praeger Publishers
521 Fifth Avenue
New York, NY 10175
(212) 599–8400

Export/Import Traffic Management Forwarding
Alfred Murr.
1979. 6th ed. rev. and
enlarged. 659p. $22.50.
Subject heading: Freight forwarders
Library of Congress Call Number: HE5999.A3 M8 1979

Updates and revises sections from the 1977 fifth edition that were affected by changes in law, general orders, and trade practice.
Cornell Maritime Press
Post Office Box 456
Centerville, MD 21617
(301) 758-1075

Export Management

Edited by Michael R. Czinkota and George Tesar.
1982. 295p. $27.95.
Subject heading: Export marketing—Addresses, essays, lectures
Library of Congress Call Number: HF1009.5 .E933 1982

Presents an international view of export management developed at the International Symposium on Exporting sponsored by Georgetown University and the Organization of American States. The book is divided into four parts, with Part One presenting studies of underlying behavioral factors that motivate export activities of smaller firms. Part Two presents findings concerning the export activities of multinational corporations. The issues of export planning and strategy are covered in Part Three, while Part Four provides an evaluation of export research.
Praeger Publishers
521 Fifth Avenue
New York, NY 10175
(212) 599–8400

Export Marketing Management

C.G. Alexandrides and George P. Moschis.
1977. 179p. $26.95.
Subject heading: Export marketing
Library of Congress Call Number: HF1009.5 .A44

Guide providing information for small- and medium-sized businesses on developing an export market. Contains descriptions and assessments of the government and commercial sources of information needed by businessmen. Also provides explanations on how to analyze the sources of information and develops evaluation models of alternative export markets.
Praeger Publishers
521 Fifth Avenue
New York, NY 10175
(212) 599–8400

Export Policy: A Global Assessment

Edited by Michael R. Czinkota and George Tesar.
1982. 175p. $21.95.
Subject heading: Foreign trade promotion—Addresses, essays, lectures
Library of Congress Call Number: HF1417.5 .E95 1982

This three-part book covers the conceptual and empirical material necessary for the formulation of public export policies. Part One contains a discussion of factors that caused increased concern over export policy.

The extent, effects, and problems of current governmental export-promotion programs are discussed in Part Two. Part Three provides an examination of possible future developments in export policy and an evaluation of main concerns.
Praeger Publishers
521 Fifth Avenue
New York, NY 10175
(212) 599–8400

Export Strategy: Markets and Competition
Nigel Piercy.
1982. 272p. $30.00.
Subject heading: Export marketing
Library of Congress Call Number: HF1009.5 .P44 1982

Presents an approach to exporting that differs from those adopted in many textbooks—particularly with regard to the advocacy of key market concentration and nonprice competition. Other distinguishing features include the provision of operational checklists and an up-to-date bibliography of exporting and closely related areas.
Allen and Unwin
Nine Winchester Terrace
Winchester, MA 01890
(617) 729–0830

Federal Regulation of International Business
Stuart S. Malawer.
1980. $285.00.
Subject heading: Foreign trade regulation—United States

A complete condensed summary of U.S. laws affecting international trade, current legislation, regulations, and treaties. The two existing volumes are updated by loose leaf. A third volume is now being prepared.
National Chamber Foundation
1615 H Street, N.W.
Washington, DC 20006
(202) 659–6077

Financial Policy Workshops: The Case of Kenya
$12.50.
Subject heading: Finance—Kenya
Library of Congress Call Number: HG187.5.K4 F55

Offers a series of workshops on Kenya used as case study in the institute's course on financial analysis and policy for officials of fund member countries.

International Monetary Fund
Publications Unit, Room C-200
700 19th Street, N.W.
Washington, DC 20431
(202) 477–2945

The Financing of Exports and Imports: A Guide to Procedures

1980. 48p. Free.
Subject heading: Export credit
Library of Congress Call Number: HG3745 .M67 1980

Morgan Guaranty Trust Company
23 Wall Street
New York, NY 10015
(212) 483–2323

Foreign Exchange Dealer's Handbook

Raymond G.F. Coninx.
$21.00.

Practical aspects and figures of foreign exchange trading are covered.
Pick Publishing Corporation
21 West Street
New York, NY 10006
(212) 425–0591

Foreign Exchange Management in Multinational Firms

Vinh Quang Tran.
1980. 238p. $31.95.
Subject heading: Foreign exchange problem
Library of Congress Call Number: HG3851 .T7

UMI Research Press
Ann Arbor, MI 48109

Foreign Exchange Review

Free.

Manufacturers Hanover Trust Company
Foreign Exchange Advisory Service
350 Park Avenue
New York, NY 10022
(212) 350–3300

Foreign Market Entry Strategies
F.R. Root
1982. 303p.
Subject heading: Export marketing
Library of Congress Call Number: HF1009.5 .R595 1982

A basic handbook for both small and large companies on how to enter foreign markets. Provides explanations of foreign-market-entry strategies, market research, export marketing, licensing, foreign investment, selecting the right market, and so on.
AMACOM Publishing Divisions
American Marketing Associations
135 West 50th Street
New York, NY 10020
(212) 586–8100

Foreign Trade Marketplace
Edited by George J. Schultz.
1977. 1st ed. 662p. $78.00.
Subject heading: Commerce—Handbooks, manuals, etc.
Library of Congress Call Number: HF1010 .F67

Gale Research Company
Book Tower
Detroit, MI 48226
(313) 961–2242

Foreign Trade of the People's Republic of China 1974–1978
1979. $7.00.
Subject heading: China—Commerce
Library of Congress Call Number: HF3836.5 .S72a

European Community Information Center
Suite 707
2100 M Street, N.W.
Washington, DC 20037
(202) 862–9500

The Fund Agreement in the Courts
2 vols. $20.00/set.

Contains discussions of cases in which the fund's Articles of Agreement have had a bearing on issues before international and national courts (volume 1, 1962; volume 2, 1982).

International Monetary Fund
Publications Unit, Room C-200
700 19th Street, N.W.
Washington, DC 20431
(202) 477–2945

Global Guide to International Business
David Hoopes.
1982. $45.00.
Subject heading: Commerce—Information services—Directories
Library of Congress Call Number: HF54.5 .H66

Contains names and addresses of relevant private, national, and international organizations and government bureau and information agencies dealing with international business. Describes kinds of information and services each provides.
Facts on File, Inc.
460 Park Avenue, South
New York, NY 10016
(212) 683–2244

Growth and Organizational Change in the Multinational Firm
John M. Stopford.
1980. 197p. $18.00.
Subject heading: Corporations, American
Library of Congress Call Number: HD2755.5 .S84 1980

Arno Press
Three Park Avenue
New York, NY 10016
(212) 725–2050

A Guide for Using the Foreign Exchange Market
Townsend Walker.
1981. 372p. $23.95.
Subject heading: Foreign exchange
John Wiley and Sons, Inc.
605 Third Avenue
New York, NY 10158
(212) 850–6418

Guidelines for the Use of Consultants by World Bank Borrowers and by the World Bank as Executing Agency
1981. Free.

Covers policies and procedures dealing with the use of consultants by bank borrowers and by the bank as executing agency for the United Nations Development Programme.
World Bank
1818 H Street, N.W.
Washington, DC 20433
(202) 477–1234

Industrial Strategy for Late Starters: The Experience of Kenya, Tanzania and Zambia
Ravi Gulhati and Uday Sekhar.
1981. 63p. $3.00.
Subject heading: Kenya—Industries; Tanzania—Industries; Zambia—Industries
Library of Congress Call Number: HC865 .G83

The scope and nature of industrialization in three African countries are assessed and the industrial development during the last twenty-five years is summarized. Also, the issues facing these countries as they plan future industrial policies are explored.
World Bank Headquarters
1818 H Street, N.W.
Washington, DC 20433
(202) 477–1234

Internal Migration in Developing Countries
Michael P. Todaro.
1980. 106p. $17.10.
Subject heading: Underdeveloped areas—Migration, Internal
Library of Congress Call Number: HB1951 .T63

Causes and consequences of internal migration affecting rural, urban economic, and social development are presented.
International Labor Office
Suite 330A
1750 New York Avenue, N.W.
Washington, DC 20006
(202) 376–2315

International Accounting and Multinational Enterprises
Jeffrey S. Arpan and Lee H. Radebaugh.
1981. 400p. $21.50.
Subject heading: International business enterprises—Accounting
Library of Congress Call Number: HF5686.I56 A76

Warren, Gorham and Lamont, Inc.
210 South Street
Boston, MA 02111
(617) 423–2020

International Banking and Finance
Robert D. Fraser.
Loose leaf for updating. $26.00/vol. 1; $35.00/vol. 2.
Subject heading: International finance
Library of Congress Call Number: HG3881 .F7117

Volume 1 covers the entire subject of international banking and finance, used as a ready reference and for staff development and training. Volume 1 gives an overview. Volume 2 includes interest rates in key markets and their relationships between LIBOR and SIBOR. Describes details of Eurodollar transactions, structure of international credits, and so on.
R & H Publishers
Box 3532
Georgetown Post Office
Washington, DC 20007

International Bonds
Frederick G. Fisher.
199p. $85.00.
Subject heading: Bonds

Practical, nonacademic guide covering such topics as how a new bond issue is syndicated and offered, who the borrowers and investors are, the many currency sectors, investment alternatives, floating-rate notes and hybrid bonds, equity convertibles, underwriting, issuing and listing, and so on.
Beverly Dewar, Marketing Manager
Euromoney Publications
Nestor House
Playhouse Yard
London EC4V 5EX England

International Business
R. Hal Mason, Robert R. Miller, Dale R. Weigel
1981. 2nd ed. $22.95.
Subject heading: International business enterprises—Management
Library of Congress Call Number: HD62.4 .M37 1981b

John Wiley and Sons, Inc.
605 Third Avenue
New York, NY 10158
(212) 850–6418

International Business: Environments and Operations
John D. Daniels, Ernest W. Ogram, Jr., and Lee H. Radebaugh.
1982. 703p. $19.95.
Subject heading: International business enterprises
Library of Congress Call Number: HD2755.5 .D35 1982

Addison-Wesley Publishing Company, Inc.
Jacob Way
Reading, MA 01867
(617) 944–3700

International Business: Introduction and Essentials
Donald A. Ball and Wendall H. McCulloch, Jr.
559p.
Subject heading: International business enterprises—Management
Library of Congress Call Number: HD62.4 .B34 1982

Business Publications
Suite 240
200 Chisholm Place
Plano, TX 75075
(214) 422–4389

International Business and Multinational Enterprises
Stefan H. Robock, Kenneth Simmonds, and Jack Zwick.
1977. 738p. $21.95.
Subject heading: International business enterprises—Management
Library of Congress Call Number: HD69.I7 R63 1977

Richard D. Irwin, Inc.
1818 Ridge Road
Homewood, IL 60430
(312) 798–6000

Multinational Business Finance
David K. Eiteman and Arthur I. Stonehill.
1982. 3rd ed. 721p.
Subject heading: International business enterprises—Finance
Library of Congress Call Number: HG4027.5 .E36 1982

Addison-Wesley Publishing Company, Inc.
Jacob Way
Reading, MA 01867
(617) 944–3700

International Business Finance: An Annotated Bibliography
Raj Aggarwal.
1982. $19.95.

Annotated bibliography of international business finance with index for easy cross-reference, inclusive through July 1978.
Praeger Publishers
521 Fifth Avenue
New York, NY 10175
(212) 599–8413

International Business Strategy and Administration
John Fayerweather.
1978. 2nd ed. 547p. $22.50.
Subject heading: International business enterprises—Management
Library of Congress Call Number: HD62.4 .F39 1982

Ballinger Publishers
54 Church Street
Cambridge, MA 02138
(617) 492–0070

International Capital Markets
99p. $65.00.
Subject heading: Bonds, foreign

Study providing a comprehensive description of available instruments in the world's national and international money and capital markets. Topics covered include fixed-interest bonds, money-market instruments and related securities, and floating-rate securities.
Marketing Manager, Euromoney Publications
Nestor House
Playhouse Yard
London EC4V 5EX England

International Codes of Conduct for Business: Some Legal Implications
1981. $10.00.

An overview is provided of the possible legal effects of codes drafted or being drafted by UNCTAD, the United Nations, the OECD, and the

ILO. Explains the major challenge to the world trade and investment system caused by the emergence of permanent rules for corporate behavior.
U.S. Council for International Business
1212 Avenue of the Americas
New York, NY 10036

International Commercial Banking Management
James L. Kammert.
403p. $24.95.
Subject heading: Banks and banking, international
Library of Congress Call Number: HG3881 .K27

Provides organized guidelines for the management of banking services in the international sector. Discusses banking skills, operations, credit and office-management procedures. Also presents useful information concerning banking schools and common forms of credit extension.
AMACOM Publishing Divisions
American Management Associations
135 West 50th Street
New York, NY 10020
(212) 586–8100

International Dimensions of Marketing
Vern Terpstra.
1981.
Subject heading: Export marketing
Library of Congress Call Number: HF1009.5 .T415

Kent Publications
18301 Halstead Street
Northridge, CA 91325
(213) 349–5088

International Dimensions of Planning
James R. Basche.
1981. 15p. $15.00.
Subject heading: International business enterprises—Management
Library of Congress Call Number: HD62.4 .B37

The Conference Board
845 Third Avenue
New York, NY 10022
(212) 759–0900

International Economic Trends

1981. 950p. $58.00.

Subject heading: Economic history, 1971– —Collected works

Library of Congress Call Number: HC13.2 .I57

Provides information on opportunities and prospects for U.S. businesses in international commerce. Contains a compilation of current reports on the economies of ninety-three nations, with each report providing key statistical data and a narrative summary of the country's economic structure. Reports were compiled and issued jointly by the Departments of Commerce and State.

Gale Research Company
Book Tower
Detroit, MI 48226
(313) 961–2242

The International Essays for Business Decision Makers

Edited by Mark B. Winchester.

1982. $25.95.

Subject heading: International economic relations—Addresses, essays, lectures

International energy policies, political risk analysis, modernization in the Muslim world, and other topics are covered.

AMACOM Publishing Divisions
American Management Associations
135 West 50th Street
New York, NY 10020
(212) 586–8100

International Experiences in Managing Inflation

James Greene.

1977. 34p. $15.00.

Subject heading: Inflation (Finance)

Library of Congress Call Number: HG229 .G677

The Conference Board
845 Third Avenue
New York, NY
(212) 759–0900

International Financial Law

1980. 319p. $85.00.

Subject heading: Loans, foreign—Law and legislation

Library of Congress Call Number: K1094.3 .I55

Contains a detailed discussion of legal considerations involved in international finance. Topics discussed include term loan agreements, loan syndications and participations, financing, the Eurodollar market, bank lending, and so on.
Marketing Manager, Euromoney Publications
Nestor House
Playhouse Yard
London EC4V 5EX England

International Institutions in Trade and Finance
A.I. MacBean and P.N. Snowden.
1981. 255p. $11.95.
Subject heading: Financial institutions, International

Institutions discussed include the International Monetary Fund, the World Bank, the General Agreement on Tariffs and Trade, the United Nations Conference on Trade and Development, and the Organization of Economic Co-operation and Development.
Allen and Unwin
Nine Winchester Terrace
Winchester, MA 01890
(617) 729–0830

International Investing
Douglas R. Casey.
1981. $9.95.
Subject heading: International business enterprises
Everest House Publishers
424 Raritan Center
Post Office Box 978
Edison, NJ 08817
(212) 841–0800
Note: Originally published in hardcover as *The International Man* and in paperback as *The Expatriate Investor.*

International Labor Profiles
1981. 304p. $50.00.

Furnishes the first forty reports in the *Country Labor Profiles* series, published by the Bureau of International Labor Affairs, U.S. Department of Labor, 1979–1980. Provides a summary of basic economic statistics and social conditions for each nation and detailed information about each country's labor force.

Gale Research Company
Book Tower
Detroit, MI 48226
(313) 961–2242

The International Man see **International Investing.**

International Marketing
Philip R. Cateora and John M. Hess.
1979. 4th ed. 734p. $20.50.
Subject heading: Export marketing
Library of Congress Call Number: HF1009.5 .C35 1979

Richard D. Irwin, Inc.
1818 Ridge Road
Homewood, IL 60430
(313) 798–6000

International Marketing
John Fayerweather.
1970. 2nd ed. 120p. $7.95.
Subject heading: Export marketing
Library of Congress Call Number: HF1009.5 .F35 1970

Prentice-Hall, Inc.
Post Office Box 500
Englewood Cliffs, NJ 07632
(201) 592–2000

International Marketing
Simon Majaro.
1982. rev. ed.
Subject heading: Export marketing
Library of Congress Call Number: HF1009.5 .M34 1982

Allen and Unwin
Building 424
Rariton Center
Post Office Box 978
Edison, NJ 08817
(201) 225–1900

International Marketing
Vern Terpstra.
1978. 2nd ed. 610p. $22.95.

Subject heading: Export marketing
Library of Congress Call Number: HF1009.5 .T417 1978

Dryden Press
901 North Elm
Hinsdale, IL 60521
(312) 325–2985

International Marketing: Managerial Perspectives
Subhash C. Jain and Lewis R. Tucker, Jr.
1979. 518p.
Subject heading: Export marketing—Addresses, essays, lectures
Library of Congress Call Number: HF1009.5 .J34

Kent Publishing Company
Ten Davis Drive
Belmont, CA 94002

International Marketing Strategy
Edited by Hans Thorelli and Helmut Becker.
1980. rev. ed. 423p. $43.00.
Subject heading: Export marketing—Addresses, essays, lectures
Library of Congress Call Number: HF1009.5 .T485 1980

Provides an outline for determining and solving international marketing problems faced by businessmen today.
Pergamon Press
Maxwell House
Fairview Park
Elmsford, NY 10523
(914) 592–7700

International Production and the Multinational Enterprise
John H. Dunning.
1981. 439p. $18.50.
Subject heading: International business enterprises
Library of Congress Call Number: HD2755.5 .D867

Provides new explanations of international economic relations. Also contains discussions of multinationals (MNCs) and the trend toward greater participation in economic activity by MNCs.
Allen and Unwin
Nine Winchester Terrace
Winchester, MA 01890
(617) 729–0830

International Reserves, Exchange Rates, and Developing-Country Finance

1982. 160p. $19.95.

Subject heading: International finance—Congresses

Library of Congress Call Number: HG205 1982 .I55

Provides an examination of the functioning of the international monetary system in light of the explosion of liquidity and its effect on international savings and investments. Cooperation to achieve monetary stability and promote needed change are also discussed.

Lexington Books
125 Spring Street
Lexington, MA 02173
(800) 428–8071

International Technology Licensing: Compensation, Costs and Negotiation

Farok J. Contractor.

1981. 193p. $24.95.

Subject heading: Foreign licensing agreements—Cost effectiveness

Library of Congress Call Number: HF1429 .C65

Provides a methodology for negotiating a technology-transfer agreement. Also featured are comparisons of the model with actual managerial behavior in a cross-section of U.S. firms and statistical testing of revenue and cost data.

Lexington Books
125 Spring Street
Lexington, MA 02173
(800) 428–8071

Investing, Licensing and Trading Conditions Abroad

Loose leaf for updating.

Subject heading: Economic history, 1945–

The actual conditions for doing business in the world's leading markets are analyzed, and key data for fifty-six countries are provided. Annual updating for each country.

Business International Corporation
World Headquarters
One Dag Hammarskjold Plaza
New York, NY 10017
(212) 750–6300

The Law of Transnational Business Transactions
Edited by Ved P. Nanda.
1981. Loose leaf. 1 vol.
Subject heading: Commercial law—Addresses, essays, lectures
Library of Congress Call Number: K1005.6 .L38

Boardman, Clark Company, Ltd.
435 Hudson Street
New York, NY 10014
(212) 929–7500

Legal and Financial Aspects of International Business
Carol McCormick Crosswell.
1980. 350p.
Subject heading: Investments, Foreign—Law and legislation
Library of Congress Call Number: K3830.4 .C76

Oceana Publications
75 Main Street
Dobbs Ferry, NY 10522
(914) 693–5944

Major Forces in the World Economy: Concerns for International Business
John Hein.
1981. 31p.
Subject heading: Commerce
Library of Congress Call Number: HF1008 .H44

The Conference Board
845 Third Avenue
New York, NY 10022
(212) 759–0900

Management of International Advertising: A Marketing Approach
Forthcoming. *Dean M. Peebles and John K. Ryans, Jr.*

Presents the necessary framework for the successful management of an overseas advertising program.
Allyn and Bacon, Inc.
470 Atlantic Avenue
Boston, MA 02210
(617) 482–9220

Management Principles for Finance in the Multinational
David B. Zenoff.
1980. 208p. $85.00.
Subject heading: International business enterprises—Finance
Library of Congress Call Number: HG4027.5 .Z46

The challenges and opportunities for strategic management of international finance are covered. Topics discussed include financing foreign operations; corporate entry into international business; integration of foreign acquisitions; borrowing options; and so on.
Beverley Dewar, Marketing Manager
Euromoney Publications
Nestor House
Playhouse Yard
London EC4V 5EX England

Managing and Organizing Multinational Corporations
Stanley M. Davis.
1979. 516p. $59.00.
Subject heading: International business enterprises—Management—Case studies
Library of Congress Call Number: HD 69 .I7 D38 1979

Pergamon Press
Maxwell House
Fairview Park
Elmsford, NY 10523
(914) 592–7700

Managing the Multinational Subsidiary
James M. Hulbert and William K. Brandt.
1980. 196p. $22.95.
Subject heading: Subsidiary corporations—Management
Library of Congress Call Number: HD62.3 .H84

Holt, Rinehart and Winston, Inc.
383 Madison Avenue
New York, NY 10017
(212) 688–9100

Market Overseas with U.S. Government Help
11p. Free.
Subject heading: Foreign trade promotion—United States

U.S. Small Business Administration
Post Office Box 15434
Fort Worth, TX 76119
(800) 433–7212

Multinational Computer Nets
Richard H. Veith.
1981. 133p. $19.95.
Subject heading: Banks and banking, international—Data processing
Library of Congress Call Number: HG1709 .V4

The interorganizational dynamics of transborder data flow are analyzed. Contents include interorganization relations; the transborder data-flow debates; and computers, networks and banks.
Lexington Books
125 Spring Street
Lexington, MA 02173
(800) 428–8071

Multinational Corporations and Developing Countries
1979. 215p. $30.00.
Subject heading: Underdeveloped areas—International business enterprises
Library of Congress Call Number: HD2755.5 .L37

The Conference Board
845 Third Avenue
New York, NY 10022
(212) 759–0900

Multinational Corporations in Comparative Perspective
1977. 76p. $15.00.
Subject heading: International business enterprises—Management
Library of Congress Call Number: HD69.I7 L27

The Conference Board
845 Third Avenue
New York, NY 10022
(212) 759–0900

Multinational Management
David Rutenberg.
1982. 385p. $19.95.
Subject heading: International business enterprises—Management
Library of Congress Call Number: HD62.4 .R87 1982

Winthrop Publishing Company
Prentice-Hall
Englewood Cliffs, NJ 07632
(201) 592–2154

Multinational Marketing Management

Warren J. Keegan.
1980. 2nd ed. 613p.
Subject heading: Export marketing
Library of Congress Call Number: HF1009.5 .K39 1980

Prentice-Hall, Inc.
Post Office Box 500
Englewood Cliffs, NJ 07632
(201) 592–2000

Multinationals from Developing Countries

Edited by Krishna Kumar and Maxwell G. McLeod.
1981. 211p. $23.95.
Subject heading: Underdeveloped areas—International business enterprises—Case studies
Library of Congress Call Number: HD2755.5 .M8445

Discusses the growth of multinational firms from developing countries. Provides an examination of the nature of these companies, their relationships with their own and host countries, and the particular assets that allow them to compete with nations that are more industrialized.
Lexington Books
125 Spring Street
Lexington, MA 02173
(800) 428–8071

The Newly Industrializing Countries: Trade and Adjustment

Louis Turner and Neil McMullen.
1982. 328p. $35.00.
Subject heading: Underdeveloped areas—Industries—Addresses, essays, lectures
Library of Congress Call Number: HC59.7 .T87

Integrated, specially commissioned study of the trade and industrial policies followed by the older economies as they confront the challenge of newly industrializing countries of the Third World. Focuses on the industrial sectors of textiles and clothing, consumer electronics, automobiles, petrochemicals,and steel.

Allen and Unwin
Nine Winchester Terrace
Winchester, MA 01890
(617) 729–0830

North-South: A Business Viewpoint

$20.00.

Furnishes the corporate spokesman's view on the contributions of the private sector to the areas of energy, raw materials, trade, finance, and development assistance. Also shows the significant impact of development-related issues on the world environment in which U.S. business must function.
U.S. Council for International Business
1212 Avenue of the Americas
New York, NY 10036
(212) 354–4480

Peru: Major Development Policy Issues and Recommendations

1981. 220p. Includes 3 annexes, statistical appendix. $20.00.
Subject heading: Peru—Economic policy
Library of Congress Call Number: HC227 .W67 1981

Discusses Peru's severe economic and financial crisis in 1977–1978 and the stabilization–economic-recovery program implemented by the government in 1978. Also discusses the high inflation, high public-sector deficit, unemployment, widespread poverty, and other problems at present. Key policy measures necessary for future development are considered.
World Bank Headquarters
1818 H Street, N.W.
Washington, DC 20433
(202) 477–1234

Political Risk in 30 Countries
Michael K. O'Leary and William D. Coplin.
210p. $145.00.
Subject heading: International business enterprises

Study provides a specific and practical analysis of the risks of doing business in the thirty most significant countries. Presents an assessment of the risks in international business due to government restriction and instability, and explains how to integrate political-risk analysis into planning and investment decisions.

Marketing Manager, Euromoney Publications
Nestor House
Playhouse Yard
London EC4V 5EX England

Pricing Policy for Development Management
Gerald M. Meier.
$35.00.

Presents explanations of the vital elements of a price system, the functions of prices, possible policies that a government might implement in cases of market failure, and the principles of public pricing of goods and services of government enterprises. Readings cover sectors such as agriculture, industry, power, urban services, foreign trade, and employment.
Johns Hopkins University Press
Baltimore, MD 21218
(301) 338–7861

Project Financing
3rd ed. 175p. $65.00.
Subject heading: Corporations—Finance

Discusses the increase of international banks linking credits to projects to ensure the proper use of loans. Topics covered include the characteristics of project financing, the risks involved and causes of project failure, lender's recourse, legal questions, sources of finance, leases, tax implications and accounting policies.
Marketing Manager, Euromoney Publications
Nestor House
Playhouse Yard
London EC4V 5EX England

Public Finance and Economic Development: Spotlight on Jamaica
Hugh N. Dawes.
147p. $21.25.
Subject heading: Jamaica—Economic conditions—Management models
Library of Congress Call Number: HC154 .D38 1982

Public finance and the extent to which it may be altered is the principal focus of this book. It also describes the possible directions an economy is likely to move and attempts to show negative trends that must be corrected. In addition, several aspects of Jamaica's economy are discussed.

University Press of America
Post Office Box 19101
Washington, DC 20036
(301) 459–3366

Reappraising the Future of U.S. Trade with the People's Republic of China
1980. 15p. $15.00.
Subject heading: United States—Foreign economic relations—China
Library of Congress Call Number: HF1456.5.C6 R4

The Conference Board
845 Third Avenue
New York, NY 10022
(212) 759–0900

Reporting Transnational Business Operations
1980. 43p. $15.00.
Subject heading: Corporation reports—United States
Library of Congress Call Number: HG4028.B2 L44

The Conference Board
845 Third Avenue
New York, NY 10022
(212) 759–0900

Some Aspects of the Multinational Corporations' Exposure to the Exchange Rate Risk
Hassan Jadwani and T. Jadwani.
1980. 184p. $18.00.
Subject heading: International business enterprises—Finance
Library of Congress Call Number: HG4027.5 .J33 1980

Arno Press
Three Park Avenue
New York, NY 10016
(212) 725–2050

Sources of European Economic Information
Edited by Euan Blauvett and Jennifer Durlacher.
1981. $95.00.
Subject heading: Europe—Economic conditions—Bibliography
Library of Congress Call Number: Z7165.E8 S68 1982

Unipub
345 Park Avenue, South
New York, NY 10010
(212) 686–4707

Target Setting for Basic Needs
P.J. Richards and M.D. Leonor.
1982. 130p. $14.25.
Subject heading: Underdeveloped areas—Economic policy

Provides an analysis of the operations involved in the government service sectors of health, education, housing, and transportation. Also contains discussions of pertinent and acceptable forms of target setting with particular reference to developing countries.
International Labor Office
Suite 330A
1750 New York Avenue, N.W.
Washington, DC 20006
(202) 376–2315

Tax and Trade Guide Series
Free.

Over twenty-three countries are covered in this series. Each guide contains information on the country and its government, business organization, finance, employment, and taxation, and so on.
Arthur Anderson and Company
Distribution Clerk
69 West Washington
Chicago, IL 60603
(312) 580–0069

Technological Exchange, the U.S.-Japanese Experience: Proceedings of a Symposium Held on October 21, 1981
Edited by Cecil H. Uyehara.
1982. 442p. $8.25.
Subject heading: Technology transfer—Japan—Congresses
Library of Congress Call Number: T174.3 .T358

Largely composed of papers presented at the U.S.-Japan Technological Exchange Symposium and summaries of the discussions following each paper. Past technological exchange between the United States and Japan is reviewed and the management and legal implications are analyzed. Topics covered include patents, licensing, taxes, and the antitrust aspects of technological exchange.

University Press of America
Post Office Box 19101
Washington, DC 20036
(301) 459–3366

Technologies for Basic Needs

Hans Singer.
1982. 2nd ed. 158p. $17.10.
Subject heading: Underdeveloped areas—Technology
Library of Congress Call Number: T49.5 .S58

Discusses the question of how Third World countries should choose the kind of technology that is consistent with the factor endowment and development goals of the country.
International Labor Office
Suite 330A
1750 New York Avenue, N.W.
Washington, DC 20006
(202) 376–2315

Ten Years of Multinational Business

Edited by Malcolm Crawford and James Poole.
1982. 176p. $25.00.
Subject heading: International business enterprises—Addresses, essays, lectures
Library of Congress Call Number: HD2755.5 .T45 1982

Provides a summation of the recurrent challenges facing multinational corporations. Also included are four case studies on corporate decision making in an international context with particular emphasis on the examination of the specific corporate environment and management responses.
Abt Books
55 Wheeler Street
Cambridge, MA 02138
(617) 492–7100

Theory Z

William G. Ouchi.
1981. 283p. $12.95.
Subject heading: Industrial management—Japan
Library of Congress Call Number: HD70.J3 088

Addison-Wesley Publishing Company, Inc.
Jacob Way
Reading, MA 01867
(617) 944–3700

Touche Ross and Company

Touche Ross and Company provides a number of publications in the areas of accounting, taxation, finance, marketing, management, and so on for various countries throughout the world. While some are for internal use, many can be obtained by contacting:

Touche Ross and Company
Attention: Barbara Meyer
1633 Broadway
New York, NY 10019
(212) 489–1600

Tracing the Multinationals

Joan P. Curhan.
1977. 430p. $40.00.
Subject heading: Corporations, American—Statistics
Library of Congress Call Number: HD2785 .C89

Ballinger Publications
54 Church Street
Cambridge, MA 02138
(617) 492–0070

Trade Financing

Coordinated by Charles J. Gmhur.
190p. $85.00.
Subject heading: International Finance

Techniques and instruments in trade financing are described.
Marketing Manager, Euromoney Publications
Nestor House
Playhouse Yard
London EC4V 5EX England

Transnational Corporations and Developing Countries: New Policies for a Changing World Economy

1981. $6.50.
Subject heading: Underdeveloped areas—International business enterprises
Library of Congress Call Number: HD2755.5 .C635 1981

Committee for Economic Development
477 Madison Avenue
New York, NY 10022
(212) 688-2063

Transnational Mergers and Acquisitions in the United States

Sarkis J. Khoury and Franklin R. Root.
1980. 293p. $28.95.
Subject heading: Corporations, foreign—United States
Library of Congress Call Number: HD2785 .K45

Discusses the increase of cases of takeover by or merger with foreign firms in the United States. Provides an examination of the steps of the acquisition process and an analysis of the micro- and macro-effects on the firms and the U.S. economy. Models for evaluating these transactions are developed and applied.
Lexington Books
125 Spring Street
Lexington, MA 02173
(800) 428-8071

Transnational Money Management: Issues and Practices

Vincent G. Massaro.
1978. 47p. $30.00.
Subject heading: International business enterprises—Finance
Library of Congress Call Number: HG4028.I53 M37

The Conference Board
845 Third Avenue
New York, NY 10022
(212) 759-0900

United Nations

The United Nations produces a variety of highly specialized publications with a heavy emphasis on economic data.
Some examples of UN publications are:

Transnational Corporations in Advertising

Transnational Corporations in the Pharmaceutical Industry

The Activities of Transnational Corporations in the Industrial, Mining and Military Sectors of Southern Africa

Technology Assessment for Development

Manual for Evaluation of Industrial Products

Mineral Processing in Developing Countries

Institutional Arrangements in Developing Countries for Industrial and Export Finance with a View to Expanding and Diversifying Their Exports of Manufacturers and Semi-Manufacturers.

The Economic Commission for Europe and Energy Conservation: Recent Experience and Prospects

For more information contact:
United Nations Publications
Room A-3315
New York, NY 10017
(212) 244-1330

U.S. Economic Performance in a Global Perspective
1981. Free.

This study examines the economic performance of eight major industrial nations over the past twenty years.
New York Stock Exchange
Office of Economic Research
11 Wall Street
New York, NY 10005
(212) 623–3000

United States Exports in World Markets
John Hein.
1978. 19p. $15.00.
Subject heading: United States—Commerce
Library of Congress Call Number: HF3031 .H44

The Conference Board
845 Third Avenue
New York, NY 10022
(212) 759–0900

U.S. Multinationals and Foreign Governments: The Competitive Aspects
1979. $15.00.
The Conference Board
845 Third Avenue
New York, NY 10022
(212) 759–0900

Venezuelan Foreign Policy: Its Organization and Beginning
Douglas Carlisle.
1979. 208p. $10.50.
Subject heading: Foreign relations—History

Study focusing on the rule of General Vincente Gomez (1908–1935) and the foreign-relations arm of the Venezuelan government. Provides an in-depth examination of the Ministry of Foreign Affairs.
University Press of America
Post Office Box 19101
Washington, DC 20036
(301) 459–3366

Village Water Supply: Economics and Policy in the Developing World
Robert J. Saunders and Jeremy J. Warford.
1976. 279p. $21.00.
Subject heading: Underdeveloped areas—Water resource development

Discusses the problem of drinkable water supply and waste disposal in rural areas of developing countries where the majority of impoverished are located. The economic, social, financial, and administrative issues characterizing village water-supply and sanitation programs are emphasized.
Johns Hopkins University Press
Baltimore, MD 21218

Where to Find Business Information
David M. Brownstone and Gorton Carruth.
1982. 2nd ed. 632p. $45.00.
Subject heading: Industrial management—Information services
Library of Congress Call Number: HD30.35 .B76 1982

John Wiley and Sons
605 Third Avenue
New York, NY 10158
(212) 850–6418

The World Bank
1981. 12p. Free.
Subject heading: World Bank

Provides a summary of the operations of the World Bank and the International Development Association (IDA). The provision of technical assistance, and coordination, and ownership and control are explained.

World Bank Headquarters
1818 H Street, N.W.
Washington, DC 20433
(202) 477–1234

World Bank Research in Water Supply and Sanitation—Summary of Selected Publications

1980. 7p. Free.
Subject heading: Water supply—bibliography

Papers in the Water Supply and Sanitation Series are included in this bibliography. Also provides listing of the World Bank studies in Water Supply and Sanitation.
The Johns Hopkins University Press
Baltimore, MD 21218
(301) 338–7861

World Economic Outlook

1982. 154p. $11.00.
Subject heading: Economic history, 1971–
Library of Congress Call Number: HC59 .W645 1981

Information on the outlook for industrial, oil-exporting, and non-oil developing countries is provided.
Publications Unit
International Monetary Fund
Box A-100
Washington, DC 20431
(202) 477–2945

World Energy Outlook

1982. 106p. $45.00.
Subject heading: Power resources
Library of Congress Call Number: HD9502.A2 073 1977

Forecasts for oil, natural gas, coal, and other energy sources to the year 2000 are provided. Also includes more than 180 statistical tables as well as full texts of energy-policy guidelines adopted by the IEA.
OECD Publications and Information Center
1750 Pennsylvania Avenue, N.W.
Washington, DC 20006
(202) 724–1857

World Product and Income: International Comparisons of Real GDP
Irving B. Kravis, Allen Heston, and Robert Summers.
1982. 388p. $30.00.
Subject heading: National income
Library of Congress Call Number: HB141.5 .K72 1982

Provides comparisons of prices, real per-capita quantities, and final expenditure components of GDP for thirty-four countries for 1975. Equations to approximate per-capita GDP for the thirty-four countries for 1950 to 1978 are developed. Also estimates the distribution of world product by region and per-capita income class for 1975.
The Johns Hopkins University Press
Baltimore, MD 21218
(301) 338–7861

The World's Multinationals: A Global Challenge
John Hein.
1981. 10p. $15.00.
Subject heading: International business enterprises
Library of Congress Call Number: HD2755.5 .H43

The Conference Board
845 Third Avenue
New York, NY 10022
(212) 759–0900

Worldwide Foreign Investment in Manufacturing
1979.
The Conference Board
845 Third Avenue
New York, NY 10022
(212) 759–0900

Appendix: Additional Names and Addresses of Organizations Where Country and Product Data May Be Obtained

World Trade Centers

World Trade Center Argentina, Buenos Aires
Centra, S.A.
San Antonio 741–(1276)
Buenos Aires, Argentina
Cable: SAUCA-BAIRES
Telex: 18402 ARCEN
Telephone: 28–0071/6–8035–8220

Melbourne Chamber of Commerce
60 Market Street
Melbourne, Victoria 3000
Australia
Cable: COMPORT
Telephone: 626681

World Trade Centre Melbourne
Port of Melbourne Authority
29 Market Street
P.O. Box 2239T
Melbourne, Victoria
Australia 3001
Cable: HARBOR
Telex: AA34211
Telephone: 62073

Australian (Melbourne) World Trade Centre Pty. Ltd.
60 Market Street
Melbourne, Victoria 3000
Australia
Telephone: 626681

Export Promotion Bureau
122–124 Motijheel Commercial Area
Chamber Building
Dacca, Bangladesh
Cable: EXPROM, DACCA
Telex: DACCA 601
Telephone: 255001, 230500

N.V. The World Trade Center of Belgium
Markgravestraat 12
B-2000 Antwerp, Belgium
Cable: WORLTREDCENT
Telephone: 031/32.22.20

Chamber of Commerce and Industry
Markgravestratt 12
B-2000 Antwerp, Belgium
Cable: KOOPHANDEL
Telephone: 32.22.19

De Brugse Hanze
Internationale Club of West Flanders
Steenstraat 96
8000 Brugge, Belgium
Telephone: 050/33.47.99

World Trade Center Association Brussels A.S.B.L.
WTC Building
162 Boulevard Emile Jacqmain, bte 12
1000 Brussels, Belgium
Cable: WORLDTRADE BRUSSELS
Telex: 26766
Telephone: 218.05.43

Office Belge du Commerce Exterieur
World Trade Center—Tower 1
Boulevard Emile Jacqmain, 162—Box 36
1000 Brussels, Belgium
Telex: 21502 BEXPO B
Telephone: 294.44.50 or 210.45.50

International Club of Flanders
St-Pietersplein 11
9000 Ghent, Belgium
Telephone: 091.22.96.68

World Trade Centers Association Directory, 1981.

World Trade Center do Rio de Janeiro
Serviease S.A.
Rua Mexico, III—15 andar
Rio de Janeiro, Brazil 20031
Telex: NR: (021) 31299 BMTR
Telephone: NR: (021) 224–3065/
252–9524

World Trade Center de Sao Paulo
Serviease S.A.
Alameda Santos 1827—8 andar CJ.82
Sao Paulo, Brazil 001419
Telex: NR: (011) 22917 GIGO BR
NR: (011) 289–8722

World Trade Center Calgary
c/o W.T.C. World Trade Centres of
Canada Ltd.
Suite 500
90 Sparks Street
Ottawa, Ontario, Canada K1P 5B4
Cable: WELCALD
Telephone: (613) 233–5666

World Trade Centre Halifax
W.T.C. Halifax World Trade Centre
Ltd.
Suite 1300, Duke Street Tower
Scotia Square
Halifax, Nova Scotia,
Canada B3J 2N9
Telephone: (902) 429–5050

World Trade Centre Montreal
W.T.C. Montreal World Trade Center
Ltd.
1191 Mountain Street
Montreal, Quebec, Canada H3G 1Z2
Telephone: (514) 866–1352

World Trade Center Ottawa
W.T.C. World Trade Centres of
Canada Ltd.
Suite 500
90 Sparks Street
Ottawa, Ontario, Canada K1P 5B4
Cable: WELCALD
Telephone: (613) 233–5666

World Trade Centre Toronto
Toronto Harbour Commissioners
60 Harbour Street
Toronto, Ontario, Canada M5J 1B7
Cable: WORLDTRADE TORONTO
Telex: 06–219666
Telephone: (416) 863–2000

World Trade Centre Vancouver
W.T.C. World Trade Centre of
Vancouver Ltd.
P.O. Box 10020
1900–700 West Georgia Street
Vancouver 1, B.C. Canada
Cable: BOWFRIDGE
Telephone: (604) 688–0211

World Trade Centre Winnipeg
c/o W.T.C. World Trade Centres of
Canada Ltd.
Suite 500
90 Sparks Street
Ottawa, Ontario, Canada K1P 5B4
Cable: WELCALD
Telephone: (613) 233–5666

Chamber of Commerce of the Republic
of Cuba
661 21st Street
Vedado, Havana City
Cuba
c/o Cuban Interests Section
2630 16th Street, N.W.
Washington, DC 20009
Telex: 511752 CAMAR CU

World Trade Center Copenhagen
International House
Bella Center A/S
Center Boulevard
DK-2300 Copenhagen S. Denmark
Cable: BELLACENTER
Telex: IHSTM 31124
Telephone: (01) 51 88 11

Centro de Desarrollo (CENDES)
Av. Orellana
1715 Y9 De Octubre
P.O. Box 23-21
Quito, Ecuador
Telex: 2350 CENDES ED

Alexandria Shipping and Navigation Company
557 El Horreya Avenue
Glym Alexandria, Egypt
Cable: ALEXSHIP
Telex: 4029–4104
Telephone: 966660

Cairo World Trade Center
Arab International Bank
35 Abdel Khalek Sarwat Street
P.O. Box 1563
Cairo, Egypt
Cable: ARABINBANK
Telex: 2079 AIB
Telephone: 916120 and 916233

World Trade Center Port Said
Arab International Bank
35 Abdel Khalek Sarwat Street
P.O. Box 1563
Cairo, Egypt
Cable: ARABINBANK
Telex: 2079 AIB
Telephone: 916233 or 916244

World Trade Center Cologne
(WTC Verwaltungs-und Betriebsgeselischaft mbH)
Hochhaus Wienerplatz 2
D-5000 Cologne 80
Federal Republic of Germany
Telex: 8873356 WTCD
Telephone: 0221–612418

World Trade Center LaHavre
c/o Chambre de Commerce et d'Industrie du Havre
Palais de la Bourse
76600 Le Havre, France
Telephone: (35) 41.22.90

Mediterraneen World Trade Center
SOMECIN (Societé du Centre Mediterraneen de Commerce International)
2 rue Beauvau
13001 Marseille, France
Telex: CECOMEX MARSEILLE 440796
Telephone: (91) 54–22–56

World Trade Center of Paris (France)
41 rue Berger
75001 Paris, France
Cable: WORLDTRADE PARIS
Telex: 670 814 WORTRAD PARIS
Telephone: 233.61.10

Maison du Commerce International de Strasbourg (MCIS)
Immeuble "Le Concorde"
4 Quai Kleber
F 67056 Strasbourg Cedex France
Telex: ITAST 890673 (code 101)
Telephone: (88) 32.48.90

World Trade Center Athens
Chandris House
95 Akti Miaouli Piraeus
Athens, Greece

Guatexpro
National Export Promotion Center
6a. Avenida 0-60, zona 4
Torre Professional, 5to. Nivel
Guatemala City, Guatemala, C.A.
Cable: GUATEXPRO
Telex: 4128 (code) GUATEX GU
Telephone: 511821/9

Hungarian Chamber of Commerce
Kossuth Lajos Ter 6-8
Budapest H-1055
P.O. Box 106
Budapest, Hungary 1389
Cable: KAMARA BUDAPEST
Telex: 22–4745
Telephone: 314–155

World Trade Centre Hong Kong
c/o The Hongkong Land Company Ltd.
Alexandra House, 5th Floor
16–20 Chater Road
Hong Kong
Cable: LANDS HONGKONG
Telex: 75102 LANDS HX
Telephone: 5–265471

World Trade Centre, Bombay
M. Visvesvaraya Industrial Research and Development Centre
Cuffe Parade
Coleba, Bombay-5, India
Cable: VIRDCOM
Telephone: 214434,271396
Telex: 011–6846 WTCB IN

Trade Development Authority
Bank of Baroda Building
16, Parliament Street
P.O. Box 767
New Delhi, 110001, India
Telex: 2735 adept
Grams: ADEPT
Telephone: 312819

World Trade Center of Indonesia
P.T. Jakarta Land
Level 10, Wisma Metropolitan
Kav. 29, JLN. JEND. Sudirman
P.O. Box 3164/JKT
Jakarta, Indonesia
Cable: 'JAKLAND', JAKARTA
Telex: 44589 JAKLAND IA
Telephone: 584801, 584802, 584803

Shannon World Trade Centre
Shannon Airport, Co. Clare
Republic of Ireland
Cable: 'WORLDTRADE' Shannon
Telex: 24051 SWTD E1
Telephone: (061) 62504

World Trade Center Israel
Industry House
29 Hamered Street
P.O. Box 29116
Tel-Aviv, Israel
Cable: MAIS
Telex: 342651 MAIL IL
Telephone: 03–65–01 21

World Trade Center Italy
Vitale Milanofiori
20094 Assago (Milan) Italy
Cable: WORLDTRADEMILAN
Telex: 316425 SVIMI I
Telephone: 02–82–41.665

Ivorian Center of Foreign Trade
(Centre Ivorien Du Commerce Exterieur)
P.O. Box V. 68
Abidjan, Ivory Coast
Telex: 460 CICE ABIDJAN
Telephone: 32 08 33

The World Trade Center of Japan, Inc.
P.O. Box 57
World Trade Center Building
No. 4-1, 2-chome, Hammamatsu-cho
Minato-ku, Tokyo, 105 Japan
Cable: WORLDTRADE TOKYO
Telex: 242 2661 WORLDT J
Telephone: (03) 435–5651

World Trade Center Club of Japan
World Trade Center Building
No. 4-1, 2-chome, Hammamatsu-cho
Minato-ku, Tokyo, 105 Japan

World Trade Center of Korea
Korean Traders Association
10-1, 2-ka, Hoehyon-dong, Chung-Ku
C.P.O. Box 1117
Seoul, Korea
Cable: KOTRASO SEOUL
Telex: KOTRASO K24265
Telephone: 771–41

World Trade Center Kuwait
Abdul Mohsen Badr Al-Khorafi Establishment
P.O. Box No. 3539
Safat, Kuwait
Cable: MOAB
Telex: 2017 KUWAIT
Telephone: 414585

World Trade Center Beirut
P.O. Box 11. 11. 11.
Beirut, Lebanon
Cable: WORLDTRADE BEIRUT
Telex: 21762LE (TAKDOM)
Telephone: 234.664 or 291.175

World Trade Center Malaysia Sdn. Bhd.
P.O. Box 644
Kuala Lumpur 02-01, Malaysia
Cable: SUAGONG KUALA LUMPUR
Telephone: 03–87141/3

World Flower Trade Center (R-Commodity)
Oosteinde 15-17
1017 wt Amsterdam
The Netherlands

World Trade Center Amsterdam
Prinses Irenestraat 59
P.O. Box 7030
1007 JA Amsterdam
Cable: WORLDTRADER AMSTERDAM
Telex: 18888 AMTRA
Telephone: (20) 44.51.37

World Trade Center Rotterdam (Wereldhandelscentrum) N.V.
Meent 134
P.O. Box 30055
30001 DA Rotterdam
The Netherlands
Telex: 26402 WTCRO NL
Telephone: (010) 333611

World Trade Centre Auckland Inc.
Downtown Square
Customs Street West
2nd Floor
Auckland 1, New Zealand
Cable: BILDCEN
Telex: NZ21442
Telephone: Ph.30.976

Bureau of Export Promotion, Manila
6th Floor, Allied Bank Building
Ayala Avenue
Makati, Metro Manila, Philippines
Cable: MINTRADE
Telephone: 87–62–45

World Trade Center Lisbon
Av. Do Brasil N.I.
8-1700 Lisbon, Portugal
Telex: 12326 WTCLIS
Telephone: 730401

Talpel World Trade Center Co., Ltd.
Sung Shan Airport Terminal
340 Tun Hwa North Road
Taipei, Taiwan, Republic of China
Telex: 28094 TPEWTC
Telephone: 772–9111

China External Trade Development Council
201 Tunhwa North Road
Taipei 105, Taiwan
Republic of China
Cable: CETRA TAIPEI
Telex: 21676 CETRA
Telephone: (02) 752–2311

World Trade Centre Singapore
Suite 111, First Floor World Trade Centre
One Maritime Square
Singapore 0409
Republic of Singapore
Cable: TANJONG SINGAPORE
Telex: RS 34975
Telephone: 2712211

The South African Foreign Trade Organization
P.O. Box 9039
Johannesburg, 2000
South Africa

Scandinavian World Trade Center AB
Storgatan 26
S-411 38 Goteborg, Sweden
Telex: 27430 GOTCHAM S
Telephone: 031/177660

World Trade Center Basle
c/o Swiss Industries Fair, Basle
Isteinerstrasse 51
4021 Basle, Switzerland
Cable: FAIRS CH
Telex: 64074 WTCCS
Telephone: 016/26 20 29

World Trade Center Club of
Switzerland, Basle
Isteinerstrasse 51
CH-4021
Basle, Switzerland
Cable: FAIRS CH.
Telex: 64074 WTCCS
Telephone: 061/26 20 29

World Trade Center Geneva
P.O. Box 306
CH 1215 Geneva—Airport 15
Switzerland
Telex: 289 389
Telephone: (022) 989 989

FIATA (International Federation of
Freight Forwarders Association)
29, Brauerstrasse
POB 177
CH-8026 Zurich, Switzerland
Cable: FIATA
Telex: 57278
Telephone: 241.80.45

Istanbul Chamber of Commerce
Pagip Gumuspala Cad Eminonu
Istanbul, Turkey
Telex: 26682 ISTANBUL ODA
Telephone: 11–266215

World Trade Center Moscow
c/o SOVINCENTR
5 Mantuinskaya UL.
123100 Moscow USSR
Telex: 411486 SOVIN SU
Telephone: 256–6303

Dubal International Trade Centre
c/o Trade Center Management Co.,
Ltd.
P.O. Box 9292
Dubai, U.A.E.
Telex: 47474 DITC EM
Telephone: 472200

World Trade Centre London
London, E. 19AA, U.K.
Cable: WORLTRADE LDN
Telex: 884671
Telephone: 01–488 2400

World Trade Centre Manchester
Manchester World Trade Centre
Limited
Ship Canal House
King Street
Manchester, M2 4WU
United Kingdom
Cable: COMMERCE
MANCHESTER
Telex: 667822 CHACOM G
Telephone: 061 834 5891

Atlanta Merchandise Mart
Suite 2200
Peachtree Center
240 Peachtree Street, N.W.
Atlanta, GA 30303
Telephone: (404) 688–8994

The World Trade Center Baltimore
Baltimore, MD 21202
Cable: WTC BALT
Telex: 87–581
Telephone: (302) 659–4545

International Business Center of New
England, Inc.
22 Batterymarch Street
Boston, MA 02190
Telephone: (617) 542–0426

Cleveland World Trade Association
(Functioning within the International
Division of the Greater Cleveland
Growth Association)
690 Union Commerce Building
Cleveland, OH 44115
Telephone: (216) 621–3300

Rocky Mountain World Trade Center
Red Rock Canyon Project
3221 West Colorado Avenue
Colorado Springs, CO 80904
Telephone: (303) 633–9041

WTC Club, Fort Lauderdale
P.O. Box 7006
408/2701 E. Sunrise Boulevard
Fort Lauderdale, FL 33338
Telex: 51 4736 (FLEKS HALA)
ATTN. WTCC
Telephone: (305) 566–1330

Hawaii International Services Agency
State of Hawaii
Old Federal Building
335 Merchant Street, Room 248
Honolulu, HI 96813
Cable: HISAS
Telex: 7430356
Telephone: (808) 548-3048

World Trade Center Houston
Suite 1013
1520 Texas Avenue
Houston, TX 77002
Telephone: (713) 225–0968

World Trade Center Association of Orange County
P.O. Box 16836
Irvine, CA 92713
Telephone: (714) 752–4644

Jacksonville International Trade Association
Jacksonville Chamber of Commerce
Three Independent Drive
P.O. Box 329
Jacksonville, FL 32201
Telephone: (904) 353–0300

World Trade Center of Nevada, Inc.
World Executives Association
Suites 211–212
2765 South Highland Drive
Las Vegas, NV 89109
Cable: WORLDTRADE LAS VEGAS
Telex: 910–397–6910 WORLDCOMMU LSV.
Telephone: (702) 731–3216

Los Angeles World Trade Center
Suite 199
350 South Figueroa Street
Los Angeles, CA 90071
Telephone: (213) 489–3337

Execucentre International, Inc.
Suite 650
444 Brickell Avenue
Miami, FL 33131
Cable: EXECUCENTR
Telex: 519636 INTER A
Telephone: (305) 374–8300

Miami World Trade Center, Inc.
c/o SEFRIUS CORP.
600 Madison Avenue
New York, NY 10022
Telephone: (212) 593–2820

International House-WTC
P.O. Box 52020
New Orleans, LA 70152
Cable: INTHOUSE NEW ORLEANS
Telex: 682 (area code) 1235 IHWTCUW
Telephone: (504) 522–3591

International Trade Mart
Suite 2900
Two Canal Street ITM
New Orleans, LA 70130
Cable: INTERMART
Telex: WUI 682–1185 INTERMART
Telephone: (504) 529–1601

Port of New Orleans
Rivergate Convention Center
P.O. Box 60046
New Orleans, LA 70160
Cable: CENTROPORT
Telephone: (504) 522–2551

World Trade Center New York
The Port Authority of New York and New Jersey
Suite 63 West
One World Trade Center
New York, NY 10048
Cable: WORLDTRADE NEWYORK
Telex: 424747 PANYNJ (International)
TWX: 7105815057 (Domestic)
Telephone: (212) 466–8380

World Trade Center Norfolk
1600 Maritime Tower
Norfolk, VA 23510
Cable: Vast Ports-Norfolk
Telephone: (804) 622–1671

Orlando World Trade Center
World Trade Council of Central Florida, Inc.
75 E. Ivanhoe Boulevard
Orlando, FL 32802
Telephone: (305) 425–1234

The International Business Forum, Inc., Philadelphia
Suite 1960
1617 J.F. Kennedy Boulevard
Philadelphia, PA 19103
Telephone: (215) 568–2710

Columbia World Trade Center
Suite 1500
1001 Southwest Fifth Avenue
Portland, OR 97204
Telephone: (503) 228–6277

World Trade Center of San Francisco, Inc.
1170 Sacramento Street
Penthouse B
San Francisco, CA 94108
Telephone: (415) 928–3438

World Trade Center Tacoma
P.O. Box 1837
Tacoma, WA 98401
Telex: 32–7473
Telephone: (206) 383–5841

World Trade Center Montevideo
c/o World Trade Center Geneva, S.A.
P.O. Box 306
CH 1215 Geneva, Airport 15
Switzerland
Telex: 289–950
Telephone: (022) 989–989

World Trade Center de Venezuela Caracas C.A.
Pent-House Torre Europa
Av. Francisco de Miranda
Caracas, Venezuela
Telex: IFIVEN 23386
Telephone: 334985 and 330627

World Trade Center Zaire
B.P. 13.396
Kinshasa, 1, Republic of Zaire
Cable: WORLDTRADE KINSHASA
Telex: 21665 WTC ZR
Telephone: 32.029, 32.121

State Industrial-Development Agencies

Director
Industrial Development Division
Alabama Development Office
3734 Atlanta Highway
c/o State Capitol
Montgomery, AL 36130
Telephone: (205) 690–6112

Director
Alaska Department of Commerce and Economic Development
Pouch EE
Juneau, AK 99801
Telephone: (907) 586–3460

Director
International Trade
Office of Economic Planning and Development
Room 505
1700 West Washington Street
Phoenix, AZ 85007
Telephone: (602) 255–3737

Director
Department of Economic Development
Room 4C-300
One Capitol Mall
Little Rock, AR 72201
Telephone: (501) 371–2052

Director
Department of Economic and Business Development
1120 N Street
Sacramento, CA 95814
Telephone: (916) 322–5665

Director
Office of International Trade
350 South Figueroa Street
Los Angeles, CA 90071
Telephone: (213) 620–3474

Director
Colorado Department of Commerce and Development
Room 500
1313 Sherman Street
Denver, CO 80203
Telephone: (303) 839–2350

Director
International Division
Department of Economic Development
210 Washington Street
Hartford, CT 06106
Telephone: (203) 566–3842

Secretary
Department of Community Affairs and Economic Development
N. du Pont Highway
EVT Building
Dover, DE 19901
Telephone: (302) 736–4456

Executive Director
Office of Business and Economic Development
Room 201
District Building
14th and E Streets, N.W.
Washington, DC 20004
Telephone: (202) 727–6600

Chief
Bureau of Trade Development
Division of Economic Development
Department of Commerce
Collins Building
Tallahassee, FL 32301
Telephone: (904) 488–6124

Attracting Foreign Investment to the United States (Washington, D.C.: U.S. Department of Commerce, International Trade Administration, 1981), pp. B-1 to B-4.

Director
International Trade Division
Department of Industry and Trade
1400 North Omni International
Atlanta, GA 30303
Telephone: (404) 656–3577

Administrator
Hawaii International Services Agency
Department of Planning and Economic Development
Financial Plaza of the Pacific, #910
130 Merchant Street
Honolulu, HI 96813
Telephone: (808) 548–4621 or 548–3048

Director
State of Idaho
Office of International Trade
P.O. Box 790
Boise, ID 83701
Telephone: (208) 334–2470

Manager
Business Services Division
Department of Commerce and Community Affairs
222 South College
Springfield, IL 62706
Telephone: (217) 782–6861

Director
International Trade Division
Department of Commerce
336 State House
Indianapolis, IN 46204
Telephone: (317) 232–8845

Director
Foreign Trade
Development Commission
250 Jewett Building
914 Grand Street
Des Moines, IA 50309
Telephone: (515) 281–2351

Director
Division of Development
Department of Economic Development
6th Floor
503 Kansas Avenue
Topeka, KS 66603
Telephone: (913) 296–3336

Director
International Trade
Department of Commerce
Capital Plaza Tower
Frankfort, KY 40601
Telephone: (502) 564–2170

Director
International Development
Office of Commerce and Industry
Department of Commerce
343 International Trade Mart
New Orleans, LA 70130
Telephone: (504) 568–5255

Director
Development Office
Executive Department
State House
Augusta, ME 04333
Telephone: (207) 289–2656

Director
Office of Business and Industrial Development
Department of Economic and Community Development
1748 Forest Drive
Annapolis, MD 21401
Telephone: (301) 269–3514

Director
Massachusetts Foreign Business Council
State Street Bank Building
225 Franklin Street
Boston, MA 02110
Telephone: (617) 482–9271

Director
International Division
Office of Economic Development
Department of Commerce
5th Floor, Law Building
Lansing, MI 48909
Telephone: (517) 373–3530

Commissioner
Department of Economic Development
480 Cedar Street
Saint Paul, MN 55101
Telephone: (612) 296–2755

Executive Director
Agricultural and Industrial Board
12th Floor, Sillers Building
Jackson, MS 39202
Telephone: (601) 354–6710

Director
International Business Development
Jefferson State Office Building
P.O. Box 118
Jefferson City, MO 65102
Telephone: (314) 751–3600

Director
Governor's Office of Commerce and Small Business Development
State Capitol
Helena, MT 59601
Telephone: (406) 449–3923

Industrial Consultant
Nebraska Department of Economic Development
P.O. Box 94666
301 Centennial Mall South
Lincoln, NB 68509
Telephone: (402) 471–3111

Director
Department of International Development
Capitol Complex
Carson City, NV 89710
Telephone: (702) 885–4322

Supervisor
Foreign Trade and Commercial Development
Department of Resources and Economic Development
Six Park Street
Concord, NH 03301
Telephone: (603) 271–2591

Chief
Office of International Trade
Division of Economic Development
Department of Labor and Industry
John Fitch Plaza
Trenton, NJ 08625
Telephone: (609) 292–2323

Director
International Trade Development
Department of Commerce and Industry
113 Washington Avenue
Santa Fe, NM 87503
Telephone: (505) 827–5571

Commissioner
Department of Commerce
Twin Towers
99 Washington Avenue
Albany, NY 12245
Telephone: (518) 474–4100

New York City's Office:
Acting Deputy Commissioner
New York State Department of Commerce
Division of International Commerce
230 Park Avenue
New York, NY 10017
Telephone: (212) 949–9290

Director
International Division
Department of Commerce
430 North Salisbury Street
Raleigh, NC 27611
Telephone: (919) 733–7193

Director
Business and Industrial Development Department
523 East Bismarck Avenue
Bismarck, ND 58501
Telephone: (701) 224–2810

Director
International Trade Division
Ohio Department of Economic and Community Development
P.O. Box 1001
Columbus, OH 43216
Telephone: (614) 466–5017

Director
International Trade
Department of Industrial Development
4020 North Lincoln Boulevard
Oklahoma City, OK 73105
Telephone: (405) 521–2401

Manager
International Trade
Department of Economic Development
Fifth Floor
921 S.E. Washington
Portland, OR 97205
Telephone: (503) 229–5621/ 1–800–452–7813

Director
Bureau of International Development
Department of Commerce
408 South Office Building
Harrisburg, PA 17120
Telephone: (717) 787–7190

Puerto Rico's (New York City Office):
Deputy Administration
Economic Development Administration
35th Floor
1290 Avenue of the Americas
New York, NY 10019
Telephone: (212) 245–1200

International Trade Director
Department of Economic Development
One Weybosset Hill
Providence, RI 02903
Telephone: (401) 277–2605

Manager
International Division
South Carolina State Development Board
P.O. Box 927
Columbia, SC 29202
Telephone: (803) 758–2235

Director
Industrial Development Expansion Agency
221 South Falls Central
Pierre, SD 57501
Telephone: (605) 773–5037

Director
Export Trade
Department of Economic and Community Development
1004 Andrew Jackson Building
Nashville, TN 37219
Telephone: (615) 741–2549

Director
International Development Division
Industrial Commission
P.O. Box 12728
Capitol Station
Austin, TX 78711
Telephone: (512) 472–5059, ext. 665

Director
Industrial Development Division
Office of Community and Economic Development
165 South West Temple, #200
Salt Lake City, UT 84101
Telephone: (801) 533–5325

Director
International Business
Economic Development Department
Agency of Development and Community Affairs
Pavilion Office Building
Montpelier, VT 05602
Telephone: (802) 828–3221

Director
International Trade and Development
Division of Industrial Development
1010 State Office Building
Richmond, VA 23219
Telephone: (804) 786–4486

Executive Director
Industrial Development Commission
Virgin Islands Department of
Commerce
P.O. Box 1692
Charlotte Amalie
Saint Thomas, Virgin Islands 00801
Telephone: (809) 774–1331

Manager
Trade Development
Department of Commerce and
Economic Development
312 First Avenue, N.
Seattle, WA 98109
Telephone: (206) 464–6282

Director
Governors Office of Economic and
Community Development
Rotunda Room 150
Charleston, WV 25305
Telephone: (304) 348–0190

Secretary
Department of Business Development
123 West Washington Avenue, #650
Madison, WI 53702
Telephone: (608) 266–3222

Director
Department of Economic Planning and
Development
Barrett Building
Cheyenne, WY 82002
Telephone: (307) 777–7284

U.S. State Offices in Europe

Executive Director
Alabama International Development Consortium
Schwarztorstrasse 7
3007 Bern, Switzerland
Telex: 32150 txcab ch
Telephone: 031–45.67.67

Director
State of Alaska European Office
Vesterbrogade 1A
DK-1620 Copenhagen, Denmark
Telex: 27278 mpower dk
Telephone: 01–11.33.12

Director
State of Arkansas European Office
Avenue Louise 437
bte 4
B-1050 Brussels, Belgium
Telex: 62062
Telephone: 02–649.60.24

Director
State of Connecticut European Office
Schutzenstrasse 4
D-600 Frankfurt/Main, Germany
Telex: 416067 ctdoc d
Telephone: 0611–28.20.55/56

Director
State of Florida European Office
Zeppelinstrasse 19A
D-7000 Stuttgart 1, Germany
Telex: 721698
Telephone: 0711–292782

Managing Director
State of Georgia European Office
Square de Meeus 20
B-1040 Brussels, Belgium
Telex: 23083 inse bv
Telephone: 02–512.8185/8293

Managing Director
State of Illinois European Office
5 PLACE DU Champ de Mars
bte 14
B-1050 Brussels, Belgium
Telex: 61534 illbus b
Telephone: 02–512.01.05

European Representative
State of Indiana
P.O. Box 396
Engelse Twin 17
NL-3332 SP Zwijndrecht, Netherlands
Telex: 28013 jrc nl
Telephone: 078–193531

Director of Industrial Development
State of Iowa Development Commission
Am Salzhaus 4
D-6000 Frankfurt 1, Germany
Telex: 414623
Telephone: 0611–28.38.58

Director
Commonwealth of Kentucky European Office
Avenue Louise 379
B-1050 Brussels, Belgium
Telex: 61470 keneur b
Telephone: 2–647.13.01/649.72.45

Director
European Operations
State of Louisiana
15 Avenue Victor Hugo
F-75116 Paris, France
Telex: 620893 f
Telephone: 01–502.18.00

Attracting Foreign Investment to the United States (Washington, D.C.: U.S. Department of Commerce, International Trade Administration, 1981), pp. A-1 to A-4.

Manager
State of Louisiana
Justinianstrasse 22
D-6000 Frankfurt/Main, Germany
Telex: 414561 lco d
Telephone: 0611–59.00.61

European Director
State of Maryland
Rue Defacqz 78, bte 6
B-1050 Brussels, Belgium
Telex: 64317 mareur b
Telephone: 02–539.03.00

Director
State of Massachusetts European Office
Saint Lippenslaan 66
B-2200 Borgerhout, Belgium
Telex: 35225
Telephone: 031–365695

Director
State of Michigan European Office
Rue Ducale 41
B-1000 Brussels, Belgium
Telex: 61573 miceur
Telephone: 02–51107.31/32

Director
State of Missouri
International Business Office
Emanuel-Leutze-Str. 1
D-4000 Duesseldorf 11, Germany
Telex: 858 4645 jcmo d
Telephone: 0211–59.20.25

Director
State of Montana
Old West Regional Commission
Capim Center
Rossmarkt 15
D-6000 Frankfurt 1, Germany
Telex: 412889 capim d
Telephone: 0611–205.168

Director
State of Nebraska
Old West Regional Commission
Capim Center
Rossmarkt 15
D-6000 Frankfurt 1, Germany
Telex: 412889 capim d
Telephone: 0611–205.168

Director
c/o The Port of New York and New Jersey
Talstrasse 66
Ch-8001 Zurich, Switzerland
Telex: 813788 pony ch
Telephone: 01–211.06.15

European Representative
State of New Mexico
Bleicherweg 62
CH-8039 Zurich, Switzerland
Telex: 58654 riaz ch
Telephone: 01.202.13.70

State of New York
Department of Commerce
Panton House
25 Haymarket
London SW1Y 4EN, United Kingdom
Telex: 912721 nycom g
Telephone: 01–839.50.70

Director
State of North Carolina European Office
Wasserstrasse 2
D-400 Dusseldorf, Germany
Telex: 8581846
Telephone: 0211–32.05.33

Director
State of North Dakota
Old West Regional Commission
Capim Center
Rossmarkt 15
D-6000 Frankfurt 1, Germany
Telex: 412889 capim d
Telephone: 0611–205.168

Director
State of Ohio European Office
Avenue de la Toison d'Or 21
B-1060 Brussels, Belgium
Telex: 26698
Telephone: 02–513.07.52

Director
Commonwealth of Puerto Rico
European Office
Zurich Haus
Am Opernplatz
D-6000 Frankfurt/Main, Germany
Telex: 4189257
Telephone: 0611–72.12.42/43

Director
Commonwealth of Puerto Rico
Economic Development
Calle Doctor Fleming 1
Edificio Feygon
Madrid 16, Spain
Telex: 42339
Telephone: 01–250.76.02

Director
State of South Carolina
International Centre Rogier
bte 50
B-100 Brussels, Belgium
Telex: 26593
Telephone: 02–218.3493/7775

Director
State of South Dakota
Old West Regional Commission
Capim Center
Rossmarkt 15
D-6000 Frankfurt 1, Germany
Telex: 412889 capim d
Telephone: 0611–205.168

European Director
State of Virginia
Governor's Office
Avenue Louise 479
bte 55
B-1050 Brussels, Belgium
Telex: 26695
Telephone: 02–648.61.79/00.36

Director
State of Wyoming
Old West Regional Commission
Capim Center
Rossmarkt 15
D-6000 Frankfurt 1, Germany
Telex: 412889 capim d
Telephone: 0611–205.168

Northeast Pennsylvania
Management Research and Consulting AG
Directors
Richard Wagnerstrasse 6
CH-8002 Zurich, Switzerland
Telex: 58268 sisch
Telephone: 205.05.09

Pennsylvania Southwest Association
Director
Kuckucksweg 19
D-6240 Konigstein, Germany
Telex: 410660
Telephone: 06174–1055

U.S. Export Promotion Facilities Abroad

Bonn, Federal Republic of Germany
U.S. Export Development Office
c/o American Embassy, Bonn
APO New York 09080
Telex: 08–85–624
Telephone: 011–49–228–33–00–45
Regional responsibility: West Germany (including West Berlin), Austria, Norway, Sweden, Finland, Denmark
Facilities: No on-site exhibition facilities

London, England
U.S. Export Development Office
c/o American Embassy, London
FPO New York 09510
Telex: 24196
Telephone: 011–441–629–1710
Regional responsibility: United Kingdom, Republic of Ireland
Facilities: On-site exhibition facilities

Mexico City, Mexico
U.S. Export Development Office
Calle Liverpool 31
Mexico 6, D.F.
Telex: 017–73–471 USTC–ME
Telephone: 905–591–01–55
Regional responsibility: Mexico, Central America
Facilities: On-site exhibition facilities

Milan, Italy
U.S. Export Development Office
c/o American Consultate General, Milan
APO New York 09689
Cable: US, MILANO
Telex: 330208 USIMC–I
Telephone: 011-392–46–96–451
Regional responsibility: Italy, Spain, Portugal, Switzerland, Greece, Yugoslavia, Cyprus, Turkey
Facilities: On-site exhibition facilities

Paris, France
U.S. Export Development Office
c/o American Embassy, Paris
APO New York 09777
Cable: USTRACEN, NEUILLY
Telex: USIMC–F 610731
Telephone: 011–33–1–624–33–13
Regional responsibility: France, Belgium, The Netherlands, Luxembourg
Facilities: On-site exhibition facilities

Sao Paulo, Brazil
U.S. Export Development Office
c/o American Consultate General, Sao Paulo
APO Miami 34030
Telex: USIMC 391–1125274
Telephone: 011–55–11–853–2011
Regional responsibility: Brazil, Argentina, Paraguay, Uruguay
Facilities: On-site exhibition facilities

Singapore, Singapore
U.S. Export Development Office
c/o American Embassy, Singapore
FPO San Francisco 96699
Telex: RS25079 SINGTC
Telephone: 011–65–7373100
Regional responsibility: Singapore, Malaysia, Indonesia, Thailand, Philippines, Bangladesh, Burma, India, Nepal, Pakistan, Sri Lanka
Facilities: On-site exhibition facilities

Sydney, Australia
U.S. Export Development Office
c/o American Consulate General, Sydney
APO San Francisco 96209
Telex: AA 27619
Telephone: 011–61–2–9290977
Regional responsibility: Australia, New Zealand, Fiji, New Guinea
Facilities: On-site exhibition facilities

A Basic Guide to Exporting (Washington, D.C.: U.S. Department of Commerce, International Trade Administration, 1981), pp. 97–99.

Tokyo, Japan
U.S. Export Development Office
c/o American Embassy, Tokyo
APO San Francisco 96503
Cable: USTRACEN TOKYO
Telex: 2722446
Telephone: 011–81–3–987–2441
Regional responsibility: Japan, Hong Kong, Korea
Facilities: On-site exhibition facilities

Miami, Florida
U.S. Export Development Office
Suite 100
8125 N.W. 53rd Street
Miami, FL 33166
Telex: 810 848 4187
Telephone: (305) 350–4913
Regional responsibility: Barbados, Bolivia, Chile, Colombia, Dominican Republic, Ecuador, French Guinea, Guyana, Haiti, Jamaica, Peru, Suriname, Trinidad, Tobago
Facilities: On-site exhibition facilities

Middle East/North Africa
Office of Export Promotion
Room 6319
U.S. Department of Commerce
14th and Constitution Avenue, N.W.
Washington, DC 20230
Telephone: (202) 377–4961
Regional responsibility: Tunisia, United Arab Emirates, Yemen, People's Democratic Republic of Yemen, Qatar, Saudi Arabia, Syria, Algeria, Bahrain, Egypt, Iran, Israel, Iraq, Jordan, Kuwait, Lebanon, Libya, Morocco, Oman

Sub-Sahara Africa
Office of Export Promotion
Room 6319
International Trade Administration
U.S. Department of Commerce
14th and Constitution Avenue, N.W.
Washington, DC 20230
Telephone: (202) 377–1209
Regional responsibility: Angola, Benin, Botswana, Burundi, Cameroon, Central African Republic, Chad, Congo, Dji Bouti, Ethiopia, Equatorial Guinea, Gabon, Guinea-Bissau, Ivory Coast, Kenya, Lesotho, Liberia, Madagascar, Malawi, Mali, Mauritania, Maruitius, Mozambique, Niger, Nigeria, Rwanda, Senegal, Sierra Leone, Somalia, South Africa, Sudan, Swaziland, Tanzania, Togo, Uganda, Upper Volta, Zaire, Zambia, Zimbabwe

American Institute in Taiwan (AIT)
The Trade Center in Taipei is operated by the American Institute of Taiwan, a private, nonprofit corporation.
American Trade Center
261 Nanking East Road
Sec. 3, Taipei, Taiwan
Telex: 23890 USTRADE
Telephone: 011–86–2–781–2171
Facilities: On-site exhibition facilities

U.S. Address:
American Institute in Taiwan
1700 North Moore Street
Arlington, VA 22209
U.S. Telex: 65468 AITW
U.S. Telephone: (703) 525–8474

Associations, Organizations, and Trade Bodies Involved in Foreign Trade

Advisory Council on Japan-U.S. Economic Relations (U.S. Section)
Chamber of Commerce of the United States
International Division
1615 H Street
Washington, DC 20062
Telephone: (202) 659–3054

Air Freight Association of America
Suite 607
1730 Rhode Island Avenue, N.W.
Washington, DC 20036
Telephone: (202) 293–1030

The American Arbitration Association
140 West 51st Street
New York, NY 10020
Telephone: (212) 848–4000

American Institute of Marine Underwriters
14 Wall Street
New York, NY 10005
Cable Address: Amertute
Telex: 129245
Telephone: (212) 233–0550

American Institute of Merchant Shipping (AIMS)
1625 K Street, N.W.
Washington, DC 20006
Telephone: (202) 783–6440

American Society of International Executives
Suite 1532
1315 Walnut Street
Philadelphia, PA 19107
Telephone: (215) 567–2600

The American ASEAS Trade Council, Inc. (AATC)
Suite 501
40 East 49th Street
New York, NY 10017
Telephone: (212) 688–2755

Asian-U.S. Business Council (U.S. Section)
Chamber of Commerce of the United States
International Division
1615 H Street, N.W.
Washington, DC 20062
Telephone: (202) 659–6117

Association of American Chambers of Commerce in Latin America
1615 H Street, N.W.
Washington, DC 20062
Telephone: (202) 659–3055

Association of International Management Companies
c/o Tradecom International, Inc.
Room 333
26260 Euclid Avenue
Euclid, OH 44132
Cable: TRADINT CLV
Telex: 985277 TRADINT CLV
Telephone: (216) 261–7172

Association of Trade Chamber Executives, Inc.
200 Madison Avenue
New York, NY 10016
Telephone: (212) 561–2029

Some of the names in this list were obtained from the 77th edition of *Exporters' Encyclopedia*. A more detailed list can be found in that publication: *Exporters' Encyclopedia*. 77th ed. (New York, N.Y.: Dun and Bradstreet International, Ltd., 1982.

Brazil-U.S. Business Council (U.S. Section)
Chamber of Commerce of the United States
International Division
1615 H Street, N.W.
Washington, DC 20062
Telephone: (202) 659–3055

The Business Roundtable
Suite 2222
200 Park Avenue
New York, NY 10017
Telephone: (212) 682–6370

Chamber of Commerce of the United States
1615 H Street, N.W.
Washington, DC 20062
Telephone: (202) 659–6000

Committee on Canada-United States Relations (U.S. Section)
Chamber of Commerce of the United States
International Division
1615 H Street, N.W.
Washington, DC 20062
Telephone: (202) 659–3054

The Council of the Americas
684 Park Avenue
New York, NY 10021
Telephone: (212) 628–3200

Department of Commerce
International Trade Administration
14th Street and Constitution Avenue, N.W.
Washington, DC 20230
Telephone: (202) 377–3808

Department of State
Bureau of Economic and Business Affairs
2201 C Street, N.W.
Washington, DC 20520
Telephone: (202) 632–0354

East-West Trade Council
Suite 670
1700 Pennsylvania Avenue, N.W.
Washington, DC 20006
Telephone: (202) 393–6240

Export-Import Bank of the United States
811 Vermont Avenue, N.W.
Washington, DC 20571
Telephone: (202) 566–2117

Far-East-America Council of Commerce and Industry
1270 Avenue of the Americas
New York, NY 10020
Telephone: (212) 265–6375

FCIB-NACM Corporation (formerly Foreign Credit Interchange Bureau)
475 Park Avenue, South
New York, NY 10016
Telephone: (212) 725–1700

Federal Trade Commission
Pennsylvania Avenue at Sixth Street, N.W.
Washington, DC 20580
Telephone: (202) 523–3625

Foreign Credit Insurance Association
Ninth Floor
One World Trade Center
New York, NY 10048
Telephone: (212) 432–6200

Inter-American Development Bank
308 17th Street, N.W.
Washington, DC 20557
Telephone: (202) 634–8152

International Advertising Association, Inc.
475 Fifth Avenue
New York, NY 10017
Telephone: (212) 684–1583

International Chamber of Commerce
38, Cours Albert ler
Paris 75008, France
Telex: 650770
Telegram: Incomerc Paris
Telephone: 261–85–97

International Executives Association, Inc.
Suite 1014
122 East 42nd Street
New York, NY 10017
Telephone: (212) 661–4610

International Maritime Bureau (IMB)
Maritime House
No. 1, Linton Road
Barking, Essex IG118HH, England
Telex: 895 6492 IMB LDNG
Telephone: 01.591 3000

International Monetary Fund
700 19th Street, N.W.
Washington, DC 20431
Telephone: (202) 477–7000

International Trade Centre (UNCTAD/GATT)
4, Route des Morillons
CH-1211, Geneva 22
Switzerland

National Association of Export Management Companies, Inc.
200 Madison Avenue
New York, NY 10016
Telephone: (212) 561–2025

National Association of Manufacturers
1776 F Street, N.W.
Washington, DC 20006
Telephone: (202) 626–3800

National Committee on International Trade Documentation
30 East 42nd Street
New York, NY 10017
Cable: INTRADOCUM
Telephone: (212) 687–6261

The National Council for U.S.-China Trade
Suite 350
1050 17th Street, N.W.
Washington, DC 20036
Telephone: (202) 828–8300

National Customs Brokers and Forwarders Association of America, Inc.
Suite 1109
One World Trade Center
New York, NY 10048
Telephone: (212) 432–0050

National Export Traffic League, Inc.
234 Fifth Avenue
New York, NY 10001
Telephone: (212) 697–5895

National Foreign Trade Council, Inc.
Room 530
10 Rockefeller Plaza
New York, NY 10020
Telephone: (212) 581–6420

Office of the United States Trade Representative
1800 G Street, N.W.
Washington, DC 20506
Telephone: (202) 395–4647

Organization of American States
Washington, DC 20006
Telephone: (202) 331–1010

Organization for Economic Cooperation and Development
1750 Pennsylvania Avenue, N.W.
Washington, DC 20006
Telephone: (202) 724–1857

Overseas Private Investment Corporation
1129 20th Street, N.W.
Washington, DC 20527
Telephone: (202) 632–1804

Overseas Sales and Marketing Association of America
3500 Devon Avenue
Chicago, IL 60659
Telephone: (312) 679–6070

The Pan American Society of the U.S., Inc.
680 Park Avenue
New York, NY 10021
Telephone: (212) 744–6868

President's Export Council
Washington, DC 20230
Telephone: (202) 377–5719

Retail Credit Company
P.O. Box 4081
Atlanta, GA 30302
or
P.O. Box 427
Grand Central Station
New York, NY 10017

Small Business Administration Office of International Trade
1441 L Street, N.W.
Washington, DC 20416
Telephone: (202) 653–6600

United States Council of the International Chamber of Commerce
1212 Avenue of the Americas
New York, NY 10036
Telex: 14–8361 New York
Telephone: (212) 354–4480

U.S. Department of Commerce
Industry and Trade Administration
14th Street and Constitution Avenue, N.W.
Washington, DC 20230

U.S. Department of Commerce
Office of Minority Business Enterprise
14th Street and Constitution Avenue, N.W.
Washington, DC 20230

U.S.-European Community Conference on Agriculture
Chamber of Commerce of the United States
International Division
1615 H Street, N.W.
Washington, DC 20062
Telephone: (202) 659–2022

U.S. International Trade Commission
701 E Street, N.W.
Washington, DC 20004
Telephone: (202) 523–0161

U.S./Foreign Commercial Service Overseas Posts

The U.S. and Foreign Commercial Service (US/FCS), the U.S. Commerce Department's commercial representation staff overseas, provides overseas marketing information/assistance to American companies and assists U.S. companies that have employees stationed overseas by providing commercial intelligence and government-relations activities.

Algeria, Algiers
Four Chemin Cheich Bachir Brahimi
B.P. Box 549 (Alger-Gare)
Telex: 52064
Telephone: 601425/255/186/716/828
Workweek: Saturday–Wednesday

Argentina, Buenos Aires
4300 Colombia, 1425
APO Miami 34034
Telex: 18156 USICA
Telephone: 774–7611/8811/9911

Australia, Canberra
Moonah Pl., Canberra, A.C.T. 2600
APO San Francisco 96404
Telex: AA62104
Telephone: (062) 73–3711

Australia, Melbourne
24 Albert Road
South Melbourne, Victoria 3205
APO San Francisco 96405
Telex: 7130982+
Telephone: (03) 699–2244

Australia, Sydney
36th Floor
T&G Tower
Hyde Park Square
Park and Elizabeth Streets
Sydney 2000, N.S.W.
APO San Francisco 96209
Telephone: 264–7044

Australia, Sydney
U.S. International Marketing Center
4 Cliff Street
Milsons Point
Sydney, N.S.W. 2061
Telephone: (02) 929–0977

Australia, Perth
246 Saint George's Terrace
Perth, WA 6000
Telex: 7193848+
Telephone: (09) 322–4466

Austria, Vienna
IX Boltzmanngasse 16 A-1091
Telex: 74634
Telephone: (222) 31–55–11

Belgium, Brussels
27 Boulevard du Regent
B-1000 Brussels
APO New York 09667
Telex: 846–21336
Telephone: (02) 513–3830

Bolivia, La Paz
Banco Popular Del Peru Building
Corner of Calles Mercado and Colon
P.O. Box 425
APO Miami 34032
Telex: BX 5240
Telephone: 350251, 350120

Business America 5 (November 15, 1982):10–13.

Brazil, Brasilia
Avenida das Nocoes, Lote 3
APO Miami 34030
Telex: 061–1091
Telephone: (061) 223–0120

Brazil, Rio de Janeiro
Avenida Presidente Wilson, 147
APO Miami 34030
Telex: 021–21466
Telephone: (02) 292–7117

Brazil, Sao Paulo
Rua Padre Joao Manoel, 933
P.O. Box 8063
APO Miami 34030
Telex: 011–22183
Telephone: (011) 881–6511

Brazil, Sao Paulo
U.S. Trade Center
Edificio Eloy Chavex
Avenida Paulista, 2439
Sao Paulo
APO Miami 34030
Telex: (011) 25274
Telephone: (011) 853–2011/2455/2778

Canada, Ottawa
100 Wellington Street
K1P 5T1
Telex: 0533582
Telephone: (613) 238–5335

Canada, Calgary, Alberta
Room 1050
615 Macleod Traid, S.E.
Calgary, Alberta, Canada T2G 4T8
Canada
Telephone: (403) 266–8962

Canada, Montreal, Quebec
Suite 1122, South Tower, Place Desjardins
P.O. Box 65
Montreal H5B 1G1, Canada
Telex: 05–268751
Telephone: (514) 281–1886

Canada, Toronto, Ontario
360 University Avenue
M5G 1S4, Canada
Telex: 065–24132
Telephone: (416) 595–1700

Canada, Vancouver, British Columbia
1199 West Hastings Street
Vancouver B.C. V6E 24Y, Canada
Telephone: (604) 685–4311

Chile, Santiago
Codina Building
1343 Agustinas
APO Miami 34033
Telex: 40062–ICA–CL
Telephone: 710133/90 and 710326/75

China, Beijing
Guang Hua Lu 17
Department of State
Washington, DC 20520
Box 50
FPO San Francisco 96659
Telephone: 52–2033

China, Guangzjhou
Dong Fang Hotel Box 100
FPO San Francisco 96659
Telephone: 69900 ext. 1000

China, Shanghai
1469 Huai Hai Middle Road
Box 200
FPO San Francisco 96659
Telephone: 379–880

Colombia, Bogota
Calle 37, 8-40
APO Miami 34038
Telex: 44843
Telephone: 285–1300

Costa Rica, San Jose
Avenida 3 and Calle 1
APO Miami 34020
Telephone: 33–11–55

Czechoslovakia, Prague
Trziste 15-12548 Praha
Amembassy Prague
c/o Amcongen
APO New York, 09757
Telex: 121196 AMEMBC
Telephone: 53 66 41/8

Denmark, Copenhagen
Dag Hammarskjoids Alle 24
2100 Copenhagen O or APO New York 09170
Telex: 22216
Telephone: (01) 42 31 44

Dominican Republic, Santo Domingo
Corner of Calle Cesar Nicolas Penson and Calle Leopoldo Navarro
APO Miami 34041
Telex: 3460013
Telephone: 682–2171

Ecuador, Quito
120 Avenida Patria
APO Miami 34039
Telex: 02–2329 USICAQ ED
Telephone: 548–000

Ecuador, Guayaquil
9 de Octubre y Garcia Moreno
APO Miami 34039
Telex: 04–3452 USICAG ED
Telephone: 511–570

Egypt (Arab Republic of), Cairo
5 Sharia Latin America
Box 10
FPO New York 09527
Telex: 93773
Telephone: 28219, 774666
AMEMB workweek: Sunday–Thursday

Finland, Helsinki
Itainen Puistotie 14A
APO New York 09664
Telex: 121644 USEMB SF
Telephone: 171931

France, Paris
2 Avenue Gabriel
75382 Paris Cedex 08
APO New York 09777
Telex: 650–221
Telephone: 296–1202, 261–8075

France, Paris
U.S. International Marketing Center
123 Charles de Gaulle 92200 Neuilly
Telex: 610731
Telephone: 624–3313

France, Paris
U.S. Mission to the Organization for Economic Cooperation and Development (USOECD)
19 Rue de Franqueville, 75016 Paris
Telephone: 524–9764

Federal Republic of Germany, Bonn
Deichmannsaue, 5300 Bonn 2
APO New York 09080
Telex: 885–452
Telephone: (0228) 339–3390

Federal Republic of Germany
U.S. Export Development Office
c/o U.S. Embassy Bonn

Federal Republic of Germany, Dusseldorf
Cecillenalle 5, 4000 Duesseldorf 30
Box 515
APO New York 09080
Telex: 8584246
Telephone: (0211) 49 00 81

Federal Republic of Germany, Frankfurt AM Main
Siesmayerstrasse 21 6000 Frankfurt
APO New York 09757
Telex: 412589 USCOND
Telephone: (0611) 740071; after hours (0611) 745004

Federal Republic of Germany, Hamburg
Alsterufer 27/28, 2000 Hamburg 36
APO New York 09215
Telex: 21377
Telephone: (040) 44 10 61

Federal Republic of Germany, Hamburg
U.S. Agricultural Trade Office
Grosse Theaterstrasse 42
Telex: 02163970 ATO D
Telephone: (040) 341207

Federal Republic of Germany, Munich
Koeniginstrasse 5
8000 Muenchen 22
APO New York 09108
Telex: 5–22697 ACGM D
Telephone: (089) 2 30 11

Federal Republic of Germany, Stuttgart
Urbanstrasse 7, 7000 Stuttgart
APO New York 09154
Telex: 07–22945
Telephone: (0711) 21 02 21

Ghana, ACCRA
Liberia and Kinbu Roads
P.O. Box 194
Telephone: 66811
Com. Office Telephone: 66125

Greece, Athens
91 Vasilissis Sophias Boulevard, or
APO New York 09253
Telex: 21–5548
Telephone: 721–2951 or 721–8401 (Area code from United States: 01130–1)

Greece
Regional Trade Development Office,
91 Vasilissis Sophias Boulevard (in Embassy)

Guatemala, Guatemala
7-01 Avenida de la Reforma
Zone 10
APO Miami 34024
Telephone: 31–15–41

Honduras, Tegucigalpa
Avenido La Paz
APO Miani 34022
Telephone: 32–3120 to 29

Hong Kong, Hong Kong
26 Garden Road
Box 30
FPO San Francisco 96659
Telephone: 239011

Hungary, Budapest
V. Szabadsag Ter 12
Am Embassy
APO New York 09757
Telex: 224–222
Telephone: 329–375

India, New Delhi
Shanti Path
Chanakyapuri 21
Telex: USCS IN 031–4589 USICA
Telephone: 690351 or 46841

India, Bombay
Lincoln House
78 Bhulabhai Desai Road
Telex: 011–6525 ACON IN
Telephone: 823611/8

Indonesia, Jakarta
Medan Merdeka Selatan 5
APO San Francisco 96356
Telex: 44218 AMEMB JKT
Telephone: 340001–9

Iraq, Baghdad
Opp. for Ministry Club (Masbah Quarter)
P.O. Box 2447 Alwiyan
Baghdad, Iraq
Telex: 2287 USINT IK
Telephone: 96138/9
Workweek: Sunday–Thursday
The Embassy was closed on June 7, 1967. The government of Belgium serves as a protective power for the United States in Iraq.

Israel, Tel Aviv
71 Hayarkon Street
APO New York 09672
Telex: 33376
Telephone: 03–654338

Italy, Rome
Via Veneto 119/A
00187 Rome
APO New York 09794
Telex: 610450 AMBRMA or 613425 AMBRMB
Telephone: (06) 4674

Italy, Rome
USIS
via Boncompagni 2
00187 Rome
Telex: 614437 or 614431 USICAR

Italy, Milan
Plazza Republica 32
20124 Milano
c/o U.S. Embassy
Box M
APO New York 09794
Telephone: (02) 652–841 through 5 Commercial Section; Via Gattamelata 5, 20149 Milano
Telephone: 498–2241/2/3

Italy, Milan
U.S. International Marketing Center (Milan)
Via Gattamelata 5 (Milan Fairgrounds)
20149 Milan
Telex: 330208 USIMC I
Telephone: 469–6451 through 4

Ivory Coast, Abidjan
5 Rue Jesse Owens
01 B.P. 1712
Telex: 3660
Telephone: 32–09–79

Japan, Tokyo
10-5 Akasaka 1-chome
Minato-ku (107)
APO San Francisco 96503
Telex: 2422118
Telephone: 583–7141

Japan, Tokyo
U.S. Trade Center
7th Floor, World Import Mart
1-3 Higashi Ikebukuro 3-chome
Toshima-ku, Tokyo 170
Telex: 2722446
Telephone: 987–2441

Japan, Osaka-Kobe
U.S. Trade Center (Osaka Office)
9th Floor Sankei Building
4-9 Umeda 2-chome
Kita-ku Osaka (530)
APO San Francisco 96503
Telex: 5623023 AMCON J (Includes American Merchandise Display)
Telephone: (06) 341–27547

Kenya, Nairobi
Moi Haile Selassie Avenue
P.O. Box 30137
APO New York 09675
Telex: 22964
Telephone: 334141

Korea, Seoul
82 Sejong-Ro
Chongro-ku
APO San Francisco 96301
Telex: AMEMB 2310B
Telephone: 722–2601 through 19

Korea
U.S. Agriculture Trade Office:
63, 1-KA
Eulchi-Ro
Choong-ku

Korea
U.S. Trade Center
c/o U.S. Embassy

Kuwait, Kuwait
P.O. Box 77 SAFAT
Telephone: 424–151 through 9
Workweek: Saturday–Wednesday

Liberia, Monrovia
111 United Nations Drive
P.O. Box 98
APO New York 09155
Telephone: 222991 through 4

Malaysia, Kuala Lumpur
A.I.A. Building
Jalan Ampang
P.O. Box 35
Telephone: 26321

Mexico, Mexico, D.F.
Paseo de la Reforma 305
Mexico 5, D.F.
Telex: 017–73–091 and 017–75–685
Telephone: (905) 553–3333

Mexico
U.S. Trade Center
31 Liverpool
Mexico 6, D.F.
Telex: 01773471
Telephone: 591–01–55

Morocco, Casablanca
8 Boulevard Moulay Youssef
Telephone: 22–41–49

Netherlands, The Hague
Lange Voorhout 102
APO New York 09159
Telex: (044) 31016
Telephone: (070) 62–49–11

Netherlands, Amsterdam
Museumplein 19
APO New York 09159
Telex: 044–16176 CGUSA NL
Telephone: (020) 790321

Netherlands, Rotterdam
Vlasmarkt 1
APO New York 09159
Telex: 044–22388
Telephone: (010) 117560

New Zealand, Wellington
29 Fitzherbert Ter, Thorndon
American Embassy
Private Bag, Wellington
FPO San Francisco 96690
Telex: NZ 3305
Telephone: 722–068

Nigeria, Lagos
2 Eleke Crescent
P.O. Box 554
Telex: 21670 USEMLA NG
Telephone: 610097

Nigeria, Kaduna
5 Ahmadu Bellow Way
P.O. Box 170
Telephone: (062) 213276

Norway, Oslo
Drammensveien 18
Oslo 2 or APO New York 09085
Telex: 18470
Telephone: 56–68–80

Pakistan, Karachi
8 Abdullah Haroon Road
Telex: 82–2–611
Telephone: 515081
Workweek: Sunday–Thursday

Panama, Panama
Avenida Balboa Y Calle 3B
Apartado 6959
R.P. 5
Box E
APO Miami 34002
Telephone: Panama 27–1777

Peru, Lima
Corner Avenidas Inca Garcilaso de la Vega and Espana
APO Miami 34031
P.O. Box 1995
Lima 100
Telephone: 286000

Philippines, Manila
1201 Roxas Boulevard
APO San Francisco 96528
Telex: 722–7366
Telephone: 598–011
Com. Off.: 395 Buendia Avenue
Extension Makati
Telephone: 818–6674

Poland, Warsaw
Aleje Ujazdowskie 29/31
American Embassy Warsaw
c/o AmConGen
APO New York 09757
Telex: 813304 AMEMB PL
Telephone: 283041–9

Poland, Warsaw
U.S. Trade Development Center (Warsaw)
Ulica Wiejska 20
Telex: 8131934 USTDO PL
Telephone: 21–45–15

Portugal, Lisbon
Avenida Duque de Louie No. 39
1098 Lisboa Codex
APO New York 09678
Telex: 12528 AMEMB
Telephone: 570102

Romania, Bucharest
Strada Tudor Arghezi 7-9 or
AmConGen (Buch)
APO New York 09757
Telex: 11416
Telephone: 12–40–40

Saudi Arabia, Jidda
Palestine Road, Ruwais
APO New York 09697
Telex: 401459 AMEMB SJ
Telephone: (02) 6670080
Com. Off.: Palestine Road (opp. Embassy)
P.O. Box 149
Telephone: (092) 6670040

Saudi Arabia, Riyadh
Sulaimaniah District P.O. Box 9041
APO New York 09038
Telex: 201363 USRIAD SJ
Telephone: (01) 464–0012
USIS: P.O. Box 865

Singapore, Singapore
30 Hill Street
Singapore 0617
FPO San Francisco 96699
Telephone: 338–0251

Singapore
U.S. Agricultural Trade Office
Liat Towers Building, 15th Floor
Orchard Road
Singapore 0923
Telex: RS 25706 TRIWHT
Telephone: 7371233

Singapore
U.S. Export Development Office (Singapore)
1st Floor Malayan Credit House
96 Somerset Road
Singapore 0923
Telex: RS 25079 (SINGTC)
Telephone: 7373–100

Spain, Madrid
Serrano 75
APO New York 09285
Telex: 27763
Telephone: 276–3400/3600

Spain, Barcelona
Via Layetana 33
APO New York 09284
Telex: 52672
Telephone: 319–9550

Sweden, Stockholm
Strandvagen 101
Telex: 12060 AMEMB S
Telephone: (08) 63.05.20

Switzerland, Bern
Jubliaeumstrasse 93
3005 Bern
Telex: 32128
Telephone: (031) 437011

Thailand, Bangkok
95 Wireless Road
APO San Francisco 96346
Telephone: 252–5040/5171
Comm. Off.: "R" Floor, Shell Building
140 Wireless Road
Telephone: 251–9260/2

Turkey, Ankara
110 Ataturk Boulevard
APO New York 09254
Telephone: 26 54 70

Turkey, Istanbul
104–108 Mesrutlyet Caddesi, Tepebasl
APO New York 09380
Telephone: 436200/09

Union of Soviet Socialist Republics, Moscow
Ulitsa Chaykovskogo 19/21/23 or
APO New York 09862
Telex: 7760 USGSO SU
Telephone: (096) 252–24–51 through 59

Union of Soviet Socialist Republics, Moscow
U.S. Commercial Office (Moscow)
Ulitsa Chaykovskogo 15
Telex: 413–205 USCO SU
Telephone: 255–48–48, 255–46–60

United Arab Emirates, Abu Dhabi
Shaikh Khalid Building
Corniche Road
P.O. Box 4009
Telex: 22229
Telephone: 361534/5
AMEMBY EM Com. Sec.
Suite 504 Universal Building
Independence Street
Telephone: 345545
Workweek: Saturday–Wednesday

United Kingdom, London, England
24/31 Grosvenor Square, W. 1A 1AE or Box 40
FPO New York 09510
Telex: 266777
Telephone: (01) 499–9000

United Kingdom, London, England
U.S. Agricultural Trade Office
101 Wigmore Street
Telex: 296009 USAGOF
Telephone: 4990024

United Kingdom
U.S. International Marketing Center (in Embassy)
Telex: 24196

Uruguay, Montevideo
Calle Lauro Miller 1776
APO Miami 34035
Telephone: 40–90–51, 40–91–26

Venezuela, Caracas
Avenida Francisco de Miranda and Avenida Principal de la Floresta
APO Miami 34037
Telex: 25501 AMEMB VE
Telephone: 284–7111/6111

Venezuela, Caracas
U.S. Agricultural Trade Office
Tower C, Centro Plaza
Los Palos Grandes Caracas
Telex: 26238 USATO VC
Telephone: 2832599

Yugoslavia, Belgrade
Kneza Milosa 50
APO New York 09757
Telex: 11529
Telephone: 645655

Zaire, Kinshasa
310 Avenue des Aviateurs
APO New York 09662
Telephone: 25881 through 6

Zimbabwe, Harare
78 Enterprise Road
Highlands, Salisbury
Telephone: 791586/7

Zimbabwe, Harare
Commercial Section
5th Floor, Century House
36 Baker Avenue, West
Telex: 4591 USFCS ZW
Telephone: 705–835

Taiwan
Unofficial commercial and other relations with the people of Taiwan are maintained through a private instrumentality, the American Institute in Taiwan, which has offices in Taipei and Kachsiung. The addresses of these offices are:
American Institute in Taiwan (Taipei Office)
7/9 Lane 134, Hsin Yi Road, Section 3
Telex: 23890 USTRADE
Telephone: 708–4151
American Institute in Taiwan (Kaohsiung Office)
88 Wu Fu 3d Road
Telephone: 221–2928

International-Trade-Administration District Offices

Albuquerque, NM 87102
Room 1015
505 Marquette Avenue, N.W.
Telephone: (505) 766–2386

Anchorage, AL 99513
P.O. Box 32
701 C Street
Telephone: (907) 271–5041

Atlanta, GA 30309
Suite 600
1365 Peachtree Street, N.E.
Telephone: (404) 881–7000

Baltimore, MD 21202
415 U.S. Customhouse
Gay and Lombard Streets
Telephone: (301) 962–3560

Birmingham, AL 32505
Suite 200–201
908 South 20th Street
Telephone: (205) 254–1331

Boston, MA 02116
10th Floor
441 Stuart Street
Telephone: (617) 223–2312

Buffalo, NY 14202
1312 Federal Building
111 West Huron Street
Telephone: (716) 846–4191

Charleston, WV 25301
3000 New Federal Office Building
500 Quarrier Street
Telephone: (304) 343–6181, ext. 375

Cheyenne, WY 82001
8007 O'Mahoney Federal Center
2120 Capitol Avenue
Telephone: (307) 772–2151 ext. 2151

Chicago, IL 60603
Room 1406 Mid-Continent Plaza Building
55 East Monroe Street
Telephone: (312) 353–4450

Cincinnati, OH 45202
10504 Federal Building
550 Main Street
Telephone: (513) 684–2944

Cleveland, OH 44114
Room 600
666 Euclid Avenue
Telephone: (216) 522–4750

Columbia, SC 29201
Strom Thurmond Federal Building
1815 Assembly Street
Telephone: (803) 765–5345

Dallas, TX 75242
Room 7A5
1100 Commerce Street
Telephone: (214) 767–0542

Denver, CO 80202
Room 119 U.S. Customhouse
721 19th Street
Telephone: (303) 837–3246

Des Moines, IA 50309
817 Federal Building
210 Walnut Street
Telephone: (515) 284–4222

Business America 5 (October 18, 1982), inside back cover.

Detroit, MI 48226
445 Federal Building
231 West Lafayette
Telephone: (313) 226–3650

Greensboro, NC 27402
203 Federal Building
West Market Street
P.O. Box 1950
Telephone: (919) 378–5345

Hartford, CT 06103
Room 610-B
Federal Building
450 Main Street
Telephone: (203) 244–3530

Honolulu, HI 96850
4106 Federal Building
300 Ala Moana Boulevard
P.O. Box 50026
Telephone: (808) 546–8694

Houston, TX 77002
2625 Federal Building
515 Rusk Street
Telephone: (713) 226–4231

Indianapolis, IN 46204
357 U.S. Courthouse and Federal Office Building
46 East Ohio Street
Telephone: (317) 269–6214

Jackson, MS 39213
Suite 3230
300 Woodrow Wilson Boulevard
Telephone: (601) 960–4388

Little Rock, AR 72201
Room 635
320 West Capitol Avenue
Telephone: (501) 378–5794

Los Angeles, CA 90049
Room 800
11777 San Vincente Boulevard
Telephone: (213) 824–7591

Louisville, KY 40202
Room 636B
U.S. Post Office and Courthouse Building
Telephone: (502) 582–5066

Memphis, TN 38103
Room 710
147 Jefferson Avenue
Telephone: (901) 521–3213

Miami, FL 33130
Room 821
City National Bank Building
25 West Flagler Street
Telephone: (305) 350–3267

Milwaukee, WI 53202
605 Federal Office Building
517 East Wisconsin Avenue
Telephone: (414) 291–3473

Minneapolis, MN 55401
218 Federal Building
110 South Fourth Street
Telephone: (612) 725–2133

New Orleans, LA 70130
Room 432 International Trade Mart
Two Canal Street
Telephone: (504) 589–6546

New York, NY 10278
37th Floor
Federal Office Building
26 Federal Plaza
Foley Square
Telephone: (212) 264–0634

Okalahoma City, OK 73105
4024 Lincoln Boulevard
Telephone: (405) 231–5302

Omaha, NB 68102
Empire State Building
First Floor
300 South 19th Street
Telephone: (402) 221–3664

Philadelphia, PA 19106
9448 Federal Building
600 Arch Street
Telephone: (215) 597–2866

Phoenix, AZ 85073
2950 Valley Bank Center
201 North Central Avenue
Telephone: (602) 261–3285

Pittsburgh, PA 15222
2002 Federal Building
1000 Liberty Avenue
Telephone: (412) 644–2850

Portland, OR 97204
Room 618
1220 S.W. Third Avenue
Telephone: (503) 221–3001

Reno, NV 89502
Room 152
1755 East Plum Lane
Telephone: (702) 784–5203

Richmond, VA 23240
8010 Federal Building
400 North Eighth Street
Telephone: (804) 771–2246

St. Louis, MO 63105
120 South Central Avenue
Telephone: (314) 425–3302

Salt Lake City, UT 84101
Room 340
U.S. Post Office and Courthouse Building
350 South Main Street
Telephone: (801) 524–5116

San Francisco, CA 94102
Room 15205 Federal Building
Box 36013
450 Golden Gate Avenue
Telephone: (415) 556–5860

San Juan, Puerto Rico, 00918
Room 659 Federal Buidling
Chardon Avenue
Telephone: (809) 753–4555 ext. 555

Savannah, GA 31412
222 U.S. Courthouse
P.O. Box 9746
125-29 Bull Street
Telephone: (912) 944–4204

Seattle, WA 98109
706 Lake Union Building
1700 Westlake Avenue, North
Telephone: (206) 442–5616

Trenton, NJ 08608
240 West State Street
Eighth Floor
Telephone: (609) 989–2100

Department of Commerce Programs

Trade Complaint Service: Provides help to the international businessman in settling trade disputes with foreign firms.

Trade Fairs and Solo Exhibitions: The Department of Commerce has U.S. exhibitions at many international trade fairs. They also provide "solo" exhibitions in areas where there are no suitable trade fairs.

Trade Opportunities Program: Provides the U.S. businessman with current detailed opportunities on export trade leads. The two services available through this program are the TOP *Notice Service*, which provides U.S. companies with sales leads for specific product categories from particular overseas markets. The other service is the TOP *Bulletin*, a weekly grouping of all trade deals received from U.S. Foreign Service Posts and is primarily of interest to companies interested in export sales leads for broad ranges of products.

U.S. Specialized Trade Missions: Small groupings of American companies (twelve or less) that are promoting similar products. Relatively low-cost programs are used heavily by small- to medium-sized firms.

Automated Information-Transfer System: An automated information system that offers current international marketing data to the international businessman. Provides specific export-sales leads and many basic facts on foreign customers.

Foreign Traders Index Data Tape Service: Can be used only by organizations with computer facilities. Provides magnetic tapes with information on countries covered by the Foreign Traders Index.

WITS/Worldwide Information and Trade System: A computer-based information system that provides leads of potential business contacts; offers to export or import specific products; current statistics; schedules on various promotion events; tips on how to get started in exporting; financial information; and product information.

The Agent Distributor Service: Overseas commercial officers can identify up to six foreign firms that show interest in a specific U.S. business proposal. This program assists the firm in identifying potential foreign agents or distributors.

Business Counseling Services: Personal counseling services provided to the international businessman both at the Department of Commerce in Washington, D.C., or at any of the Department's District Offices. Offers guidance on every phase of international trade.

Business-Sponsored Promotions: Provides facilities to trade associations and individual firms when no regular exhibitions are scheduled. Promotions may include sales meetings, seminars, or conferences.

Catalog Exhibitions: Provides the small firm with an opportunity to promote its product overseas through the presentation of its sales literature. These promotions are held in Foreign Service post commercial libraries or at various exhibition sites.

Foreign Buyer Program: Designed to assist the U.S. firm in making contact with foreign buyers visiting the United States. Itineraries are arranged, appointments made, plant visits scheduled, and so on. The program encourages foreign buyers to visit U.S. trade shows.

International Trade Administration District Offices: Located throughout the United States (see accompanying list for addresses), these offices supply the international businessman with the Department of Commerce publications needed for doing business overseas as well as supplying counseling to the international businessman, providing seminars, and sponsoring many other programs for companies doing business overseas.

New Product Information Service: Provides, in booklet form, a short description of new products. Distributed to the Commerce Department's Foreign Commercial Service posts overseas.

Product Marketing Service: Provides a well-equipped base from which to operate while doing business overseas for the American exporter traveling abroad. For a minimal fee, the U.S. Export Development Offices will provide the exporter with office space (up to five days); free local telephone service; audiovisual equipment; a market briefing; a list of key business prospects; and assistance in obtaining secretarial and interpreter services.

Seminar Program: Seminars that focus on the mechanics of exporting and staged throughout the United States.

Foreign Embassies in the United States

Embassy of *Afghanistan*
2001 24th Street, N.W.
Washington, DC 20008

Embassy of *Algeria*
2118 Kalorama Road, N.W.
Washington, DC 20008

Embassy of *Argentina*
1600 New Hampshire Avenue, N.W.
Washington, DC 20009

Embassy of *Australia*
1601 Massachusetts Avenue, N.W.
Washington, DC 20036

Embassy of *Austria*
2343 Massachusetts Avenue, N.W.
Washington, DC 20008

Embassy of *Bahamas*
Suite 865
600 New Hampshire Avenue, N.W.
Washington, DC 20037

Embassy of *Bahrain*
2600 Virginia Avenue, N.W.
Washington, DC 20037

Embassy of *Bangladesh*
3421 Massachusetts Avenue, N.W.
Washington, DC 20007

Embassy of *Barbados*
2144 Wyoming Avenue, N.W.
Washington, DC 20008

Embassy of *Belgium*
3330 Garfield Street, N.W.
Washington, DC 20008

Embassy of *Benin*
2737 Cathedral Avenue, N.W.
Washington, DC 20008

Embassy of *Bolivia*
3014 Massachusetts Avenue, N.W.
Washington, DC 20008

Embassy of *Botswana*
Suite 404
4301 Connecticut Avenue, N.W.
Washington, DC 20008

Embassy of *Brazil*
3006 Massachusetts Avenue, N.W.
Washington, DC 20008

Embassy of *Bulgaria*
50 East 42nd Street
New York, NY 10017

Embassy of *Burma*
2300 S Street, N.W.
Washington, DC 20008

Embassy of *Burundi*
2717 Connecticut Avenue, N.W.
Washington, DC 20012

Embassy of *Cameroon*
2349 Massachusetts Avenue, N.W.
Washington, DC 20008

Embassy of *Canada*
1746 Massachusetts Avenue, N.W.
Washington, DC 20036

Embassy of *Capte Verde*
1120 Connecticut Avenue, N.W.
No. 300
Washington, DC 20036

Embassy of the *Central African Republic*
1618 22nd Street, N.W.
Washington, DC 20008

A Basic Guide to Exporting (Washington, D.C.: U.S. Department of Commerce, International Trade Administration, 1981), pp. 114–119.

Embassy of *Ceylon*
(See Embassy of *Sri Lanka*)

Embassy of *Chad*
Suite 410
2600 Virginia Avenue, N.W.
Washington, DC 20037

Embassy of *Chile*
1732 Massachusetts Avenue, N.W
Washington, DC 20036

Embassy of *China (People's Republic of)*
2300 Connecticut Avenue, N.W.
Washington, DC 20008

Embassy of *Colombia*
2118 Leroy Place, N.W.
Washington, DC 20008

Embassy of *Congo*
14 East 65th Street
New York, NY 10021

Embassy of *Costa Rica*
2112 S Street, N.W.
Washington, DC 20008

Embassy of *Cyprus*
2211 R Street, N.W.
Washington, DC 20008

Embassy of *Czechoslavakia*
3900 Linnean Avenue, N.W.
Washington, DC 20008

Embassy of *Dahomi*
(See Embassy of *Benin*)

Embassy of *Denmark*
3200 Whitehaven Street, N.W.
Washington, DC 20008

Embassy of *Dominican Republic*
1715 22nd Street, N.W.
Washington, DC 20007

Embassy of *East Germany*
(See Embassy of the German Democratic Republic)

Embassy of *Ecuador*
2535 15th Street, N.W.
Washington, DC 20009

Embassy of *Egypt*
2715 Connecticut Avenue, N.W.
Washington, DC 20008

Embassy of *El Salvador*
2308 California Street, N.W.
Washington, DC 20008

Legation of *Estonia*
Nine Rockefeller Plaza
New York, NY 10020

Embassy of *Ethiopia*
Suite 1018
80 Wall Street
New York, NY 10005

Embassy of the *Federal Republic of Germany*
4645 Reservoir Road
Washington, DC 20007

Embassy of *Fiji*
1629 K Street, N.W.
Washington, DC 20006

Embassy of *Finland*
2133 Wisconsin Avenue, N.W.
Washington, DC 20007

Embassy of *France*
Suite 715
2000 L Street, N.W.
Washington, DC 20036

Embassy of *Gabon*
2210 R Street, N.W.
Washington, DC 20008

Embassy of *Gambia*
1785 Massachusetts Avenue, N.W.
Washington, DC 20036

Embassy of the *German Democratic Republic*
1717 Massachusetts Avenue, N.W.
Washington, DC 20036

Embassy of *Ghana*
2460 16th Street, N.W.
Washington, DC 20009

Embassy of *Grenada*
Suite 802
1101 Vermont Avenue, N.W.
Washington, DC 20005

Embassy of *Great Britain*
3100 Massachusetts Avenue, N.W.
Washington, DC 20008

Embassy of *Greece*
2211 Massachusetts Avenue, N.W.
Washington, DC 20008

Embassy of *Guatemala*
2220 R Street, N.W.
Washington, DC 20008

Embassy of *Guinea*
2112 Leroy Place, N.W.
Washington, DC 20008

Embassy of *Guinea-Bissau*
Suite 604
211 East 43rd Street
New York, NY 10017

Embassy of *Guyana*
2490 Tracy Place, N.W.
Washington, DC 20008

Embassy of *Haiti*
4400 17th Street, N.W.
Washington, DC 20011

Embassy of *Honduras*
4301 Connecticut Avenue, N.W.
Washington, DC 20008

Hong Kong Office/British Embassy
3100 Massachusetts Avenue, N.W.
Washington, DC 20008

Embassy of *Hungary*
2401 Calvert Street, N.W.
Washington, DC 20008

Embassy of *Iceland*
2022 Connecticut Avenue, N.W.
Washington, DC 20008

Embassy of *India*
2107 Massachusetts Avenue, N.W.
Washington, DC 20008

Embassy of *Indonesia*
2020 Massachusetts Avenue, N.W.
Washington, DC 20036

Embassy of *Iraq*
1801 P Street, N.W.
Washington, DC 20036

Embassy of *Ireland*
2234 Massachusetts Avenue, N.W.
Washington, DC 20008

Embassy of *Israel*
1621 22nd Street, N.W.
Washington, DC 20008

Embassy of *Italy*
1601 Fuller Street, N.W.
Washington, DC 20009

Embassy of *Ivory Coast*
2424 Massachusetts Avenue, N.W.
Washington, DC 20008

Embassy of *Jamaica*
1666 Connecticut Avenue, N.W.
Washington, DC 20009

Embassy of *Japan*
2520 Massachusetts Avenue, N.W.
Washington, DC 20008

Embassy of *Jordon*
2319 Wyoming Avenue, N.W.
Washington, DC 20008

Embassy of *Kenya*
2249 R Street, N.W.
Washington, DC 20008

Embassy of *Korea*
2320 Massachusetts Avenue, N.W.
Washington, DC 20008

Embassy of *Kuwait*
2940 Tilden Street, N.W.
Washington, DC 20008

Embassy of *Laos*
2222 S Street, N.W.
Washington, DC 20008

Legation of *Latvia*
4325 17th Street, N.W.
Washington, DC 20008

Embassy of *Lebanon*
2560 28th Street, N.W.
Washington, DC 20009

Embassy of *Lesotho*
1601 Connecticut Avenue, N.W.
Washington, DC 20009

Embassy of *Liberia*
5201 16th Street, N.W.
Washington, DC 20011

Legation of *Lithuania*
2622 16th Street, N.W.
Washington, DC 20009

Embassy of *Luxembourg*
2200 Massachusetts Avenue, N.W.
Washington, DC 20008

Embassy of *Madagascar*
2374 Massachusetts Avenue, N.W.
Washington, DC 20008

Embassy of *Malawi*
1400 20th Street, N.W.
Washington, DC 20036

Embassy of *Malaysia*
2401 Massachusetts Avenue, N.W.
Washington, DC 20008

Embassy of *Mali*
2130 R Street, N.W.
Washington, DC 20008

Embassy of *Malta*
2017 Connecticut Avenue, N.W.
Washington, DC 20008

Embassy of *Mauritania*
2129 Leroy Place, N.W.
Washington, DC 20008

Embassy of *Mauritius*
4301 Connecticut Avenue, N.W.
Washington, DC 20009

Embassy of *Mexico*
2829 16th Street, N.W.
Washington, DC 20009

Embassy of *Morocco*
1601 21st Street, N.W.
Washington, DC 20009

Embassy of *Nepal*
2131 Leroy Place, N.W.
Washington, DC 20008

Embassy of *Netherlands*
4200 Linnean Avenue, N.W.
Washington, DC 20008

Embassy of *New Zealand*
37 Observatory Circle, N.W.
Washington, DC 20008

Embassy of *Nicaragua*
1627 New Hampshire Avenue, N.W.
Washington, DC 20009

Embassy of *Niger*
2204 R Street, N.W.
Washington, DC 20008

Embassy of *Nigeria*
2201 M Street, N.W.
Washington, DC 20037

Embassy of *Norway*
2720 34th Street, N.W.
Washington, DC 20008

Embassy of *Oman*
2342 Massachusetts Avenue, N.W.
Washington, DC 20008

Embassy of *Pakistan*
2315 Massachusetts Avenue, N.W.
Washington, DC 20008

Embassy of *Panama*
2862 McGill Terrace, N.W.
Washington, DC 20008

Embassy of *Papua New Guinea*
1140 19th Street, N.W.
Washington, DC 20036

Embassy of *Paraguay*
2400 Massachusetts Avenue, N.W.
Washington, DC 20008

Embassy of *Peru*
1700 Massachusetts Avenue, N.W.
Washington, DC 20036

Embassy of *Philippines*
1617 Massachusetts Avenue, N.W.
Washington, DC 20036

Embassy of *Poland*
1640 16th Street, N.W.
Washington, DC 20009

Embassy of *Portugal*
2310 Tracy Place, N.W.
Washington, DC 20008

Embassy of *Qatar*
600 New Hampshire Avenue, N.W.
Washington, DC 20037

Embassy of *Romania*
1607 23rd Street, N.W.
Washington, DC 20008

Embassy of *Rwanda*
1714 New Hampshire Avenue, N.W.
Washington, DC 20009

Embassy of *Saudi Arabia*
Suite 428
1155 15th Street, N.W.
Washington, DC 20036

Embassy of *Senegal*
2112 Wyoming Avenue, N.W.
Washington, DC 20008

Embassy of *Seychelles*
Eighth Floor
201 East 42nd Street
New York, NY 10017

Embassy of *Sierra Leone*
1701 19th Street, N.W.
Washington, DC 20009

Embassy of *Singapore*
1824 R Street, N.W.
Washington, DC 20009

Embassy of *Somalia*
Suite 710
600 New Hampshire Avenue, N.W.
Washington, DC 20037

Embassy of *South Africa*
Suite 300
2555 M Street, N.W.
Washington, DC 20037

Embassy of *Spain*
2558 Massachusetts Avenue, N.W.
Washington, DC 20008

Embassy of *Sri Lanka*
2148 Wyoming Avenue, N.W.
Washington, DC 20008

Embassy of *Sudan*
1019 19th Street, N.W.
Washington, DC 20036

Embassy of *Suriname*
Suite 711
2600 Virginia Avenue, N.W.
Washington, DC 20037

Embassy of *Swaziland*
4301 Connecticut Avenue, N.W.
Washington, DC 20008

Embassy of *Sweden*
600 New Hampshire Avenue, N.W.
Washington, DC 20037

Embassy of *Switzerland*
2900 Cathedral Avenue, N.W.
Washington, DC 20008

Embassy of *Syria*
2215 Wyoming Avenue, N.W.
Washington, DC 20037

Embassy of *Tanzania*
2139 R Street, N.W.
Washington, DC 20037

Embassy of *Thailand*
2300 Kalorama Road, N.W.
Washington, DC 20008

Embassy of *Togo*
2208 Massachusetts Avenue, N.W.
Washington, DC 20008

Embassy of *Trinidad and Tobago*
1708 Massachusetts Avenue, N.W.
Washington, DC 20036

Embassy of *Tunisia*
2408 Massachusetts Avenue, N.W.
Washington, DC 20008

Embassy of *Turkey*
2523 Massachusetts Avenue, N.W.
Washington, DC 20008

Embassy of *Uganda*
5909 16th Street, N.W.
Washington, DC 20011

Embassy of the *Union of Soviet Socialist Republics*
1825 Phelps Place, N.W.
Washington, DC 20008

Embassy of the *United Arab Emirates*
Suite 740
600 New Hampshire Avenue, N.W.
Washington, DC 20037

Embassy of *Upper Volta*
5500 16th Street, N.W.
Washington, DC 20011

Embassy of *Uruguay*
1918 F Street, N.W.
Washington, DC 20006

Embassy of *Venezuela*
2445 Massachusetts Avenue, N.W.
Washington, DC 20015

Embassy of *West Germany* (See Embassy of the *Federal Republic of Germany*

Embassy of *Western Samoa*
Room 303
820 Second Avenue
New York, NY 10017

Embassy of *Yemen*
600 New Hampshire Avenue, N.W.
Washington, DC 20037

Embassy of *Yugoslavia*
2410 California Street, N.W.
Washington, DC 20008

Embassy of *Zaire*
1800 New Hampshire Avenue, N.W.
Washington, DC 20009

Embassy of *Zambia*
2419 Massachusetts Avenue, N.W.
Washington, DC 20008

Embassy of *Zimbabwe*
2852 McGill Terrace, N.W.
Washington, DC 20008

Ports Representation in Europe

Port of Long Beach, California
Director
Neptune Shipping Agency, Inc.
3 Carlisle Avenue
London EC3N 2ET, England
Telex: 884060
Telephone: 01–480.65.22

Georgia Ports Authority
European Director
Rungsdorferstrasse 53
P.O. Box 20 03 31
D-53 BONN/2 BAD
Godesberg, Germany
Telex: 885691 gpa d
Telephone: 02221–35.13.44

Chicago Ports Authority
Director
Place du Champ de Mars 5
bte 14
B-1050 Brussels, Belgium
Telex: 61534
Telephone: 02–512.01.05

Port of New Orleans
Director
Heideckstrasse 27
8000 Munich 19, Germany
Telex: 5213477 nola
Telephone: 089–151.036

Maryland Port Administration
European Director
Rue Ravenstein 60
B-1000 Brussels, Belgium
Telex: 26862
Telephone: 02–513.0149/5405

Massachusetts Port Authority
Director for Europe and Africa
Saint Lippenslaan 66
B-2200 Borgerhout, Belgium
Telex: 35225
Telephone: 031–365695

Port Authority of New York and New Jersey
Director
Talstrasse 66
CH-8001 Zurich, Switzerland
Telex: 53788
Telephone: 211–06.15

Delaware River Port Authority
Ameriport
Port of Wilmington, Chester, Philadelphia, Trenton, and Camden
Manager
Avenue de Roodebeek 44
B-1040 Brussels, Belgium
Telex: 23346
Telephone: 02–736.10.62

South Carolina State Port Authority
General Manager
European Office
Centre International Rogier, Passage
29
bte 50
B-1000 Brussels, Belgium
Telex: 26593
Telephone: 02–218.77.75

Virginia Port Authority
Director for Europe
Avenue Louise 479
bte 55
B-1050 Brussels, Belgium
Telex: 26695
Telephone: 02–648.80.72

Attracting Foreign Investment to the United States (Washington, D.C.: U.S. Department of Commerce, International Trade Administration, 1981), pp. A-5 to A-6.

Index

About the Author

Cynthia Ryans is an associate professor and catalog librarian at the Kent State University Library. She received the A.B.J. from the University of Kentucky and the M.L.S. from the University of Maryland, and she has done postgraduate work at Kent State University. She has held positions in the libraries of the University of Maryland, Indiana University, and the University of Kentucky. An active researcher in the area of research sources in exporting, she has written three books and has published articles in a number of library and business journals. Mrs. Ryans is currently the resources editor of the *Journal of Small Business Management.*